Apache
Desktop Reference

www.apacheref.com

Ralf S. Engelschall
Apache Software Foundation

▲ Addison-Wesley

Boston • San Francisco • New York • Toronto • Montreal
London • Munich • Paris • Madrid
Capetown • Sydney • Tokyo • Singapore • Mexico City

Covers Apache version 1.3.

The publisher offers discounts on this book when ordered in quantity for special sales. For more information, please contact:

Pearson Education Corporate Sales Division
One Lake Street
Upper Saddle River, NJ 07458
(800) 382-3419

corpsales@pearsontechgroup.com

Visit AW on the Web: www.awl.com/cseng

Library of Congress Cataloging-in-Publication (CIP) Data

Engelschall, Ralf S.
  Apache desktop reference / Ralf S. Engelschall.
    p.   cm.
  Includes bibliographical references and index.
  ISBN 0-201-60470-1
  1. Apache (Computer file: Apache Group)
  2. Web servers—Computer programs.
  I. Title.
  TK 5105.8885.A63 E54 2000
  005.7'13769—dc21   00-059355

Text printed on recycled paper
First printing, December 2000
1 2 3 4 5 6 7 8 9—MA—03 02 01 00

To Daniela,
for her patience
and loyalty

Contents

Foreword

Flexibility

When we created the Apache project five years ago, our goal was to ensure that the server-side of the Web would never be dominated by the proprietary interests of any single company. To the Apache Group, the Web is more than just a network-based application; it is the means for people to communicate across geographical and political boundaries, to cooperate in the sharing of information, and to collaborate in the creation of new works of the imagination. Web servers are the printing presses of the Internet age.

In order to achieve our goal, we needed more than just another free Web server. We needed software that is, in every way, a commercial-grade implementation of the standards that define the Web. Any feature that might distinguish one Web server over another must be achievable in Apache, using standard protocols where others might use proprietary extensions, and with the robustness expected of a professional tool.

At the same time, we also knew that a web server must be a workhorse application — subject to the anarchic nature of the Internet, and yet expected to work 24 hours a day, 7 days a week, 52 weeks a year. Being webmasters for our own sites, we knew that the greater the performance requirements, the more emphasis there must be on maintaining a small server "footprint" — the size and complexity of the software executable that acts as the brains of the web server. High-performance sites needed the ability to remove any functionality from the server that was not needed for their own resources.

When Robert Thau designed the module framework that distinguishes the Apache architecture, its purpose was to provide webmasters with the ability to include almost any feature they might want in a web server, and yet do so in a way that avoided requiring the same features to be present on every server. While keeping the core server simple, the module framework allows each server to be tailored to the specific needs of the site it serves. Flexibility.

However, flexibility doesn't come without cost. In order to properly configure and run an Apache server, a webmaster needs to be familiar with the hundreds of feature modules that are available. Furthermore, each module can define its own set of configuration directives for controlling its behavior and that of the server as a whole. Without a guide, even us core server developers would get lost in the maze of optional features that make Apache work so well across so many different sites.

What Ralf has provided, in the form of this desktop reference, is a complete guide to the features and configuration information needed to run Apache as a robust, flexible, and high-performance web server. As one of the core developers, Ralf provides a level of insight regarding the inner-workings of Apache that you won't find in a typical user manual. This is the kind of book that you want located next to every server console.

As you work with the Apache software, remember that all of this has been accomplished by a volunteer community of software developers collaborating across the Internet. Open source is shared custom software — it only comes about when individuals have the foresight to share what they do with the rest of the world. The Apache Software Foundation supports a number of open-source software projects related to Web technology, including the HTTP server project, and welcomes anyone with a desire to contribute toward the future of Apache.

> — Roy T. Fielding,
> July 2000, Irvine, California

Preface

The best way to predict
the future is to invent it.
— Alan Kay

On a monthly basis, Netcraft checks a representative set of web servers around the world to gather statistics about the server market. For its *Web Server Survey*[1] in April 2000 (see Figure 0.1 on the following page), more than 14 million web sites were contacted and their server software identified by parsing the HTTP responses.

According to Netcraft, as of April 2000, more than 60 percent of the servers were based on Apache — that is, more than 8 million web servers. Apache has been the market leader for more than three years now and has put a large distance between itself and its competitors (Microsoft Internet Information Server: 21 percent; Netscape server family and various others: less than 10 percent each). In other words, Apache is the definitive, world-leading web server software on the market and a drop in popularity is not expected in the next 12 months. On the contrary, its popularity is increasing.

Apache is the world-leading web server.

The Purpose and Audience of This Book

Most webmasters who must manage and maintain an Apache server installation are already familiar with Apache, either through the online available documentation from the *Apache Software Foundation* (ASF) or through the various Apache books on the market. The purpose of this book is to provide a concise but, fairly complete reference to the various Apache knobs and levers with which the webmaster is confronted at compile time, configuration time, and runtime. Thus the audience of this book consists of webmasters who are already familiar with Apache, but who need a reference on a daily basis.

This book is a reference for people who already know Apache under UNIX.

---

[1]`http://www.netcraft.com/survey/`

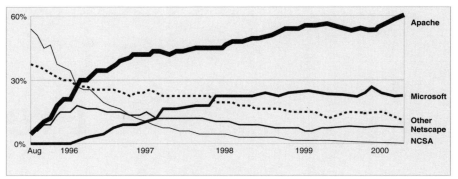

Figure 0.1: The Netcraft *Web Server Survey* through April 2000

This book does not cover all third-party modules, Apache optimization techniques, or use of Apache under non-UNIX platforms.

The book does not purport to explain Apache or to describe all referenced material in great detail. Instead, it serves as a companion to the various Apache tutorial-style books on the market. As a result, the book does not cover special topics like existing third-party modules, optimization of Apache under runtime, or use of Apache under non-UNIX platforms. If you are interested in those topics, consult one of the tutorial-style books.

Organization of This Book

This book is organized into six chapters.

Chapter 1, *Introduction*, discusses the history and evolution of the Internet, hypertext, and the World Wide Web and describes how Apache and the ASF fit into this world. This chapter is intended to provide a quick reference to historical Apache-related numbers and introduce the Apache world.

Chapter 2, *Apache Functionality*, considers the Apache program architecture, which consists of a core part and various extensional modules. A concise reference to the standard Apache modules follows this discussion. This chapter is intended to provide a compact overview of the Apache module world.

Chapters 2 and 4 are the primary reference chapters.

Chapter 3, *Building Apache*, covers building the Apache package from the distributed source codes. It first shows a typical Apache installation procedure step by step, then provides a reference to all *Apache Autoconf-style Interface* (APACI) options, and finally discusses some special configuration issues like the *Dynamic Shared Object* (DSO) facility. This chapter is intended to help you install a reasonable Apache instance.

Chapter 4, *Configuring Apache*, focuses on the runtime configuration of Apache. It introduces the gory details of the Apache configuration files and contexts, then includes a complete reference of all configuration directives provided by all standard Apache modules. This chapter is the heart of this book.

Chapter 5, *Running Apache*, discusses ways to run the Apache web server and provides a reference to all command-line options. It is intended to provide the webmaster with a quick reference for the regular Apache start-up and restart situations.

Chapter 6, *Apache Resources*, lists the various other Apache resources that you can consult to obtain details on a topic. It provides references to the most important Apache resources on the Internet.

How to Read This Book

The most reasonable approach to reading this book is to first read the non-reference parts once and then to read the remaining parts only on demand. The first reading depends on your existing skill:

■ **You are familiar with Apache in general, but you are not an expert.**

We recommend that you first read Chapter 1 for an introduction to the material, than read the first sections of Chapters 2 and 3 to refresh your knowledge of the Apache module architecture and the *APACI* facility. Next, very carefully read the first nonreference sections of Chapter 4, trying to understand how the Apache configuration contexts work. Finally, glance over the remaining chapters, which contain material that you can find later on demand.

Everyone should read at least the first part of chapter 4 as a refresher course on Apache configuration contexts. The remaining parts can then be read on demand.

■ **You are an Apache expert.**

We recommend that you first read Chapter 1 to refresh your Apache background, followed by a careful reading of the first nonreference part of Chapter 4 to refresh your knowledge of Apache configuration context handling. Finally, glance over the remaining parts of the book, which contain material that you can find later on demand.

Your subsequent readings should occur only on demand or if you are interested in more details. Refer to Chapter 2 if you are searching for details on an Apache module, Chapter 3 if you want details on APACI options, Chapter 4 if you are seeking details on particular Apache configuration directives, Chapter 5 if you are searching for a command line directive, and Chapter 6 if you need more help.

Typographic Conventions

We use *italic* text for special names and other highlighted terms. We use `constant width` text to indicate configuration directives, commands entered at the command line, and other computer code.

Companion Web Site and Feedback

This book has its own dedicated companion web site at www.apacheref.com.

This book has a companion web site at `http://www.apacheref.com/`, maintained by this book's author. Here you can find online versions of the reference materials and resource lists in this book, errata, and other information about this book and Apache.

Please address comments and questions concerning this book and its companion web site via e-mail directly to the author at `rse@apacheref.com`.

Acknowledgments

This book was sometimes nasty to write, because I wrote it at the same time that I had many very time-consuming tasks to complete for my computer science study. Additionally, while I assembled the reference information, I often had to fix bugs in the Apache source or the online documentation first. Unfortunately, this endeavor greatly delayed the creation of this book.

The greatest thanks go to my wife Daniela, because she was always very insightful and let me hack the whole day and even on weekends without complaining. She was also the person who regularly forced me to work on this book when I became lost in hacking on other things.

Additional thanks go to reviewers Mark J. Cox, Roy T. Fielding, Ken Coar, Jim Jagielski, Shane Owenby, Sander van Zoest, Stefan Winz, Gautam Guliani and Christian Reiber. I also thank Mary T. O'Brien and John Fuller from Addison-Wesley for the original idea for this book and the long-term project assistance. Finally, thanks go to Kathy Glidden and her team at Stratford Publishing Services for their help in proofreading and publishing the book.

— Ralf S. Engelschall,
July 2000, Munich, Germany

Chapter **1**

Introduction

*Apache: generous hackers from around
the world all join forces to help you
shoot yourself in the foot for free.*
— Unknown (paraphrased)

In Chapter 1, we look at the history of the World Wide Web (WWW)
by remembering its evolution out of two important fundamentals: the
global Internet, which forms the networking basis, and the hypertext concept, which is the root of the "web of documents" idea. We then look at the
the role of web servers, the Apache Group, and finally the Apache Group's
popular HTTP server project.

All topics are rounded up by historical background details, with the goal
of giving you a better understanding of Apache's evolution and its world. If
you are not interested in history (or already know the details), you can skip
this introductory chapter. When you plan to base your web business on an
Apache web server, however, it is certainly reasonable to know a little bit
more about this world first.

The World Wide Web
combines the global
dimension of the
Internet with the
associative concept of
hypertext.

1.1   History and Evolution

1.1.1   The Internet

In 1957, the USSR launched *Sputnik*, the first artificial earth satellite. In response to this event, the United States formed the *Advanced Research Projects*

Agency (ARPA) within the *Department of Defense* (DoD) to establish a U.S. lead in science and technology applicable to the military. In 1969, the U.S. DoD founded *ARPANET* to facilitate networking research, establishing a network out of four initial nodes: University of California – Los Angeles (UCLA), Stanford Research Institute (SRI), University of California – Santa Barbara (UCSB), and University of Utah (see Figure 1.1).

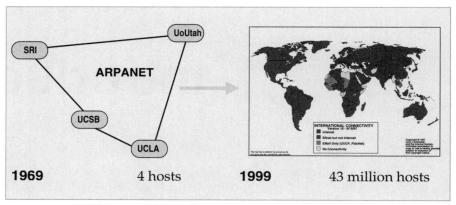

Figure 1.1: From four nodes to a covered world

This network consisted of 50 Kbps lines and used the *Network Control Protocol* (NCP), the first host-to-host protocol. Over the years, more and more hosts were connected to *ARPANET*, and the first hundred *Request for Comments* (RFC) were written to discuss and document the used protocols and software. In 1974, Vint Cerf and Bob Kahn published "A Protocol for Packet Network Interconnection," which specified in detail the design of a *Transmission Control Program* (TCP). In 1978, TCP was split into two protocols: *Transmission Control Protocol* (TCP) and *Internet Protocol* (IP).

The Internet started with 4 nodes in 1969; just 30 years later, more than 43 million nodes exist.

In 1982, the DoD declared TCP and IP (commonly known as TCP/IP) to be its official protocol suite. This move led to one of the first definitions of an "internet" as a connected set of networks, specifically those using TCP/IP, and of the "Internet" as the globally connected TCP/IP internets. In January 1983, *ARPANET* officially switched from NCP to TCP/IP, thereby creating the Internet. Explosive growth followed: In 1984, the number of hosts already broke 1,000; in 1987, it reached 10,000; in 1989, it achieved the 100,000 mark; in 1992, it was at 1,000,000; in 1996, it reached 10,000,000. As of this writing (1999), the Internet counts more than 43,000,000 hosts.[1] There is still no stagnation in sight (see also Figure 1.2 on the facing page).

---

[1]Hobbes' Internet Timeline
http://www.isoc.org/guest/zakon/Internet/History/HIT.html

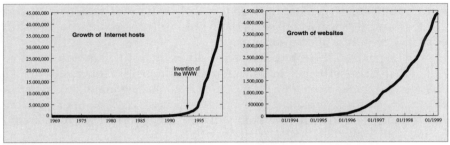

Figure 1.2: The growth of the Internet (number of connected hosts) and the World Wide Web (number of web servers)

1.1.2 The Hypertext Concept

The idea of hypertext dates back to 1945. As director of the *Office of Scientific Research and Development* under U.S. president Franklin Roosevelt, Vannevar Bush coordinated the activities of some 6,000 leading American scientists in the application of science to warfare. In his pioneering article entitled "As We May Think," published in *The Atlantic Monthly*[2] in July 1945, he proposed the creation of "memex," a device "in which an individual stores all his books, records, and communications, and which is mechanized so that it may be consulted with exceeding speed and flexibility." The "essential feature of the memex" was not only its capacities for retrieval and annotation but also those involving "associative indexing" — what today's hypertext systems term a "hyperlink."

> Hypertext is a very old concept that was reanimated and became most popular through the World Wide Web.

In 1965, Ted Nelson from *Xanadu* coined the term *hypertext*. Later, at *Brown University* (Providence, Rhode Island), Andries van Dam in 1967 created the *Hypertext Editing System* (HES) and the *File Retrieval and Editing System* (FRESS)[3] — two of the first real hypertext document systems. In 1968, Douglas C. Engelbart[4] (best known as the inventor of the computer mouse in 1963) demonstrated the *NLS* (for "oNLine System," later renamed *Augment System*) in a multimedia presentation at the *Fall Joint Computer Conference* (FJCC) in San Francisco, California. This event marked the world debut of the mouse, hypermedia, and on-screen video teleconferencing.

After this pioneering event, many systems were created over the years, all of which were highly influenced by the hypertext idea (1975: *ZOG* at Carnegie Mellon University; 1978: Aspen Movie Map by Andy Lippman from MIT; 1984: *Filevision* by Telos; 1985: *Symbolics Document Examiner* by Janet Walker; 1985: *Intermedia* by Norman Meyrowitz at Brown University; 1986: *Guide* from OWL, *NoteCards* from XeroxPARC, and so on). In 1987,

---

[2]http://www.theatlantic.com/unbound/flashbks/computer/bushf.htm
[3]http://www.stg.brown.edu/projects/hypertext/landow//HTatBrown/FRESS.html
[4]http://www.bootstrap.org/dce-bio.htm

Apple introduced *HyperCard*[5], which was invented by Bill Atkinson. HyperCard was regarded as a "milestone in the history of computing, and a shift of paradigm in educational software."

The HyperTEXT'87 conference was held in Chapel Hill, North Carolina — the first large-scale meeting devoted to the hypertext concept itself. As noted in the conference report, "Hypertext is non-sequentially linked pieces of text or other information ... The things which we can link to or from are called nodes, and the whole system will form a network of nodes interconnected with links."[6]

> Hypertext consists of nonsequentially linked pieces of data. The data that can be linked to or from are called nodes, and the whole system forms a network of nodes interconnected with links.

1.1.3 The World Wide Web

In March 1989, Tim Berners-Lee (Tim B.L.) from CERN[7] (European Laboratory for Particle Physics) wrote a document entitled "Information Management: A Proposal,"[8] in which he tried to propose answers to the question "How will we ever keep track of large projects?" This paper circulated for comments at CERN in 1990.

After approval of the idea by Mike Sendall (Tim B.L.'s boss), work started on a hypertext GUI browser and editor using the NeXTStep development environment.[9] Tim B.L. made up "WorldWideWeb" as a name for the program; later it was renamed "Nexus" to avoid confusion between the program and the abstract information space.[10] After the project was developed at CERN over two years, the World Wide Web (WWW) quickly became the first global hypertext system and the abbreviation WWW entered the public consciousness.

> After pushing the project at CERN between 1991 and 1993, the World Wide Web (WWW) quickly became the first global hypertext system.

After these initial events a fast evolution occurred, made possible by both the hypertext concept and the availability of the Internet, which represented a promising development field. Figure 1.3 on the next page tries to illustrate this evolution with a few milestones.

The client side   The client side of the WWW is controlled by two factors: the Hypertext Markup Language (HTML) and the popular browsers that form the front end to the end user and render the WWW data on the desktop. In 1993, the first HTML versions were designed; in addition, the National Center for Supercomputing Applications (NCSA) created its *Mosaic*

---

[5]http://www.apple.com/hypercard/

[6]Published in the *ACM SIGCHI Bulletin* 19, 4 (April 1988), pp. 27–35.
  Online version: http://www.sun.com/950523/columns/alertbox/ht87.html

[7]http://www.cern.ch/

[8]http://www.w3.org/History/1989/proposal.html

[9]See http://www.w3.org/People/Berners-Lee/WorldWideWeb.html for screenshots and descriptions.

[10]World Wide Web is now spelled with spaces.

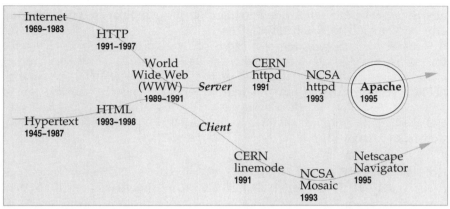

Figure 1.3: The evolution and milestones of the World Wide Web

browser, which immediately became Internet killer application number one. The popular *Netscape Navigator* later evolved from *Mosaic*; today, it rules on half of all desktops.[11] Other early browsers (for example, *Lynx*) also remain in wide use, however.

HTML, which was originally a very small SGML-based markup language, evolved over the years into a highly complex markup language (currently it is at version 4.0). Together with various companion languages and object models (for example, JavaScript, DOM), graphics formats (for example, GIF, JPEG, PNG), and multimedia data (for example, audio, video), the client side of the WWW constitutes a very colorful, complex, and sometimes even chaotic area. And especially because this area is so colorful, most people identify the WWW with just this client side and totally forget that another part exists — the server side.

> Because the client side of the WWW is so colorful, most people identify the WWW with just this part and totally forget that there is another part — the server side.

The server side The server side part is less colorful and interesting than the client-side — but only at first glance. One cannot make screenshots, see colorful icons, or click, for instance. But that is the world of Apache. Once you become familiar with it, you will recognize that it is the *really* interesting part of the WWW.

> On the server side of the WWW, one cannot make screenshots, see colorful icons, or click — but that is the world of Apache.

Here Tim Berners-Lee in 1991, and Ari Luotonen and Henrik F. Nielsen in 1993/1994, started to write the "CERN HTTP server," which was the first real web server. In 1993, Tony Sanders wrote a web server in Perl called "Plexus," and Robert McCool at NCSA wrote a competitive package in C, the "NCSA httpd."[12] This NCSA web server became very popular over the

---

[11] The other half of the desktop is controlled by Microsoft's *Internet Explorer*.

[12] "httpd" stands for "HTTP daemon," which means a stand-alone running UNIX process serving data via HTTP.

next two years, though its development and maintainance were dropped after McCool left NCSA in 1994.

Out of this situation, a group of people started to assemble patches for the NCSA httpd. After it became clear that NCSA httpd was dead, it became a nasty task to just assemble patches; in February 1995, the Apache HTTP server project was born out of these patches (hence the name "a patchy server"). Apache was initially based on NCSA httpd 1.3. The first official public Apache release appeared in April 1995 (more details are in section 1.2.2 on page 12).

Role of the HTTP server   While everyone knows HTML, most people fail to recognize HTTP (Hypertext Transfer Protocol), the workhorse of WWW network communication. This application layer protocol exists on top of TCP/IP and is used by web browsers and servers to transfer the various multimedia data behind hyperlinks. The web server accepts such HTTP connections from browsers and sends out the data queried through hyperlinks (represented as Uniform Resource Locators; see also Figure 4.1 on page 60) and various auxiliary HTTP header fields. For an illustration of this task, see Figure 1.4.

> Nowadays everyone knows HTML, but lots of people have never recognized the role played by HTTP.

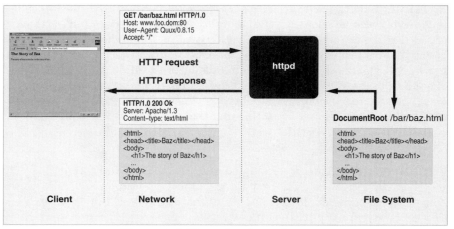

Figure 1.4: The role of a web server

Keep in mind that although this task looks easy at first (and is easy in principle), difficulties arise from not-so-obvious requirements related to high performance (a web server can be faced with thousands of HTTP requests at the same time), customization (the content providers have very different situations and requirements), portability (Apache runs on all major server platforms), reliability, and other considerations. And although Apache isn't the fastest or maximally customizable web server, its popularity comes from the fact that it provides a very good balance of these things bundled with maximum portability and reliability.

1.2 The Apache Group

The people behind the Apache web server belong to the Apache Group. If you plan to base your web business on an Apache web server, it is reasonable to learn some essentials about this group, its server project, and the organization behind it, the Apache Software Foundation.

1.2.1 A Group of Volunteers

What is the Apache Group? One of its members, Rob Hartill, once sarcastically described the Apache Group as follows:

> *The Apache Group:*
> *a collection of talented individuals who are trying*
> *to perfect the art of never finishing something.*

Perhaps this description fits the reality of the group very well. For instance, in summer 1997 the group thought (after Apache 1.2 was released) that it could quickly incorporate the recently contributed Windows NT port and release it as Apache 1.3 one or two months later, as an interim release between Apache 1.2 and the long-awaited Apache 2.0. Unfortunately, this plan failed horribly. Ultimately, the release of Apache 1.3 required seven beta versions and a development period of an entire year. So, instead of summer 1997, Apache 1.3 was released in summer 1998 . . .

One reason that Apache has been so reliable is that the Apache Group doesn't have a marketing department.

Although the developers' time plans often prove unrealistic, one should not treat this delay as a drawback. As Roy T. Fielding summarized the group's plans: "I mean releasing Apache when it is ready to be released, rather than according to an arbitrary schedule. One of the reasons Apache has been so reliable in the past is that we don't have a marketing department." Users often forget this important point.

Additionally, the work of the Apache developers should not be undervalued just because their planning is sometimes a little bit chaotic. Actually, the Apache Group developers were always very productive in their free time. Since the amalgamation of the group in 1995, developers have written approximately 70,000 lines of polished ANSI C code, released around 80 Apache versions, written more than 50,000 mails of internal correspondence, and edited in excess of 3,000 bug reports. Thus, it is actually more correct to say that the Apache Group is a collection of talented individuals who spend a great part of their *free time* trying to create the best web server money can't buy.

The Apache Group is a collection of talented individuals who spend a great part of their free time trying to create the best web server money can't buy.

Who are the members of the Apache Group?   As of April 2000, the Apache Group included the following active members (in alphabetical order):

Brian Behlendorf (USA)	Alexei Kosut (USA)
Ryan Bloom (USA)	Martin Kraemer (DE)
Ken Coar (USA)	Ben Laurie (UK)
Mark J. Cox (UK)	Rasmus Lerdorf (USA)
Lars Eilebrecht (DE)	Doug MacEachern (USA)
Ralf S. Engelschall (DE)	Aram W. Mirzadeh (USA)
Roy T. Fielding (USA)	Sameer Parekh (USA)
Tony Finch (UK)	Daniel Lopez Ridruejo (USA)
Dean Gaudet (USA)	Wilfredo Sanchez (USA)
Dirk-Willem van Gulik (IT)	Cliff Skolnick (USA)
Rob Hartill (UK)	Marc Slemko (CA)
Brian Havard (AU)	Greg Stein (USA)
Ben Hyde (USA)	Bill Stoddard (USA)
Jim Jagielski (UK)	Paul Sutton (USA)
Manoj Kasichainula (USA)	Randy Terbush (USA)

The Apache Group is a colorful bunch of totally different hackers from around the world — every one full of spirit.

The following people are Apache emeriti — that is, old group members now off doing other things:

Chuck Murcko (USA)	Robert S. Thau (USA)
David Robinson (UK)	Andrew Wilson (UK)

Additionally, many contributors from around the world have added their development effort to the Apache Group from time to time. Their help has been especially notable in the *Apache HTTP server project*.

1.2.2   The Apache HTTP Server Project

What is the Apache HTTP server project?   The HTTP server project is the Apache Group's main project. This collaborative software development effort is aimed at creating a robust, commercial-grade, featureful, and freely available source code implementation of an HTTP server. This server is well known as "the Apache." The volunteers are therefore known as "the Apache Group."

How did the Apache HTTP server project start?   Let Roy T. Fielding, another member of the Apache Group (and one of the fathers of HTTP), describe the early days of the project:

"In February 1995, the most popular server software on the Web was the public domain HTTP daemon developed by Rob McCool at the *National Center for Supercomputing Applications*, University of Illinois, Urbana-Champaign. However, development of that `httpd` had stalled after Rob left NCSA in mid-1994, and many webmasters had developed their own extensions and bug fixes that were in need of a common distribution. A small group of these webmasters, contacted via private e-mail, gathered together for the purpose of coordinating their changes (in the form of 'patches'). Brian Behlendorf and Cliff Skolnick put together a mailing list, shared information space, and logins for the core developers on a machine in the California Bay Area, with bandwidth and diskspace donated by *HotWired* and *Organic Online*. By the end of February, eight core contributors formed the foundation of the original Apache Group:

By the end of February 1995, eight core contributors had formed the foundation of the original Apache Group.

Brian Behlendorf	Roy T. Fielding	Rob Hartill
David Robinson	Cliff Skolnick	Randy Terbush
Robert S. Thau	Andrew Wilson	

with additional contributions from

Eric Hagberg	Frank Peters	Nicolas Pioch

Using NCSA httpd 1.3 as a base, we added all of the published bug fixes and worthwhile enhancements we could find, tested the result on our own servers, and made the first official public release (0.6.2) of the Apache server in April 1995. By coincidence, NCSA restarted its own development during the same period, and Brandon Long and Beth Frank of the NCSA Server Development Team joined the list in March as honorary members so that the two projects could share ideas and fixes.

Apache was originally based on NCSA httpd, version 1.3.

The early Apache server was a big hit, but we all knew that the codebase needed a general overhaul and redesign. During May–June 1995, while Rob Hartill and the rest of the group focused on implementing new features for 0.7.x (like pre-forked child processes) and supporting the rapidly growing Apache user community, Robert Thau designed a new server architecture (code-named 'Shambhala') that included a modular structure and API for better extensibility, pool-based memory allocation, and an adaptive preforking process model. The group switched to this new server base in July and added the features from 0.7.x, resulting in Apache 0.8.8 (and its brethren) in August.

After extensive beta testing, many ports to obscure platforms, a new set of documentation (by David Robinson), and the addition of many features in the form of our standard modules, Apache 1.0 was released on December 1, 1995. Less than a year after the group was formed, the Apache server passed NCSA's `httpd` as the number 1 server on the Internet."

Over the past few years, many volunteers have contributed thousands of bug fixes, cleanups, and enhancements for Apache. Their work has allowed

Apache to keep its leading market position. A few insights of this evolution follow.

	Lines of Code		
Version	**Code**	**Comments**	**Total**
1.0.5	11,551	6,099	17,650
1.1.3	18,896	9,786	28,682
1.2.6	33,526	15,715	49,241
1.3.3	52,341	24,956	77,297
1.3.12	69,646	31,041	100,687

Table 1.1: The Apache code evolution

Apache 1.3 consists of 100,000 lines of polished ANSI C code.

The evolution of Apache   The Apache web server has remained under continuous development during the past few years. Table 1.1 gives you an impression of the Apache source code basis. It lists a few major Apache release versions and the number of lines of code they include (divided into lines of comments and actual code).

Table 1.2 on the facing page summarizes the individual Apache releases in more detail. It shows the version numbers, their release dates, and the number of patches (distinguished code changes) in every release. As you can see, so far the development of Apache 1.3 has required the greatest amount of effort.

Apache 2.0 will also provide multithreading instead of the pre-forked process model of Apache 1.3. It will be not ready for production before summer 2001.

The future of Apache   As of April 2000, the Apache developers were actively working on Apache 2.0, which will provide multithreading under UNIX Operating System (UNIX) together with lots of smaller enhancements and changes. This change will allow Apache to scale better, require less system resources, and perform more quickly compared to the pre-forked process model of Apache 1.3. Before a 2.0 release version is stable enough for production environments, however, at least one more year will certainly pass. So don't be alarmed: The current stable Apache version is 1.3 — and that is the version covered in this book.

1.2.3   The Apache Software Foundation

Since 1999, the *Apache Software Foundation* (ASF) has been the official organization behind the Apache people. The ASF exists to provide organizational, legal, and financial support for Apache open-source software projects.

The foundation has been incorporated as a membership-based, not-for-profit corporation to ensure that the Apache projects continue to exist beyond the participation of individual volunteers, to enable contributions of

Date	Version	Patches	Date	Version	Patches
18-Mar-1995	0.2	1	09-Jul-1996	1.1.1	5
24-Mar-1995	0.3	1	25-Nov-1996	1.2b0	NA
02-Apr-1995	0.4	1	02-Dec-1996	1.2b1	1
10-Apr-1995	0.5.1	9	10-Dec-1996	1.2b2	18
NA-Apr-1995	0.5.2	4	23-Dec-1996	1.2b3	21
NA-Apr-1995	0.5.3	2	30-Dec-1996	1.2b4	8
NA-Apr-1995	0.6.0	11	12-Jan-1997	1.1.2	2
31-May-1995	0.6.1	5	14-Jan-1997	1.1.3	2
NA-Apr-1995	0.6.2	11	NA-Jan-1997	1.2b5	36
05-May-1995	0.6.3	NA	26-Jan-1997	1.2b6	2
NA-May-1995	0.6.4	NA	22-Feb-1997	1.2b7	38
NA-NA-1995	0.6.5	NA	07-Apr-1997	1.2b8	47
NA-NA-1995	0.7.0	NA	NA-Apr-1997	1.2b9	32
NA-NAN-1995	0.7.1	NA	28-Apr-1997	1.2b10	5
NA-NAN-1995	0.7.2	NA	28-May-1997	1.2b11	23
14-Jul-1995	0.8.0	9	16-Jun-1997	1.2.0	0
17-Jul-1995	0.8.1	3	19-Jul-1997	1.2.1	27
19-Jul-1995	0.8.2	11	23-Jul-1997	1.3a1	50
24-Jul-1995	0.8.3	8	NA-Aug-1997	1.2.2	18
26-Jul-1995	0.8.4	6	19-Aug-1997	1.2.3	4
30-Jul-1995	0.8.5	10	22-Aug-1997	1.2.4	2
02-Aug-1995	0.8.6	5	16-Oct-1997	1.3b2	99
03-Aug-1995	0.8.7	3	20-Nov-1997	1.3b3	55
08-Aug-1995	0.8.8	2	05-Jan-1998	1.2.5	17
12-Aug-1995	0.8.9	20	19-Feb-1998	1.2.6	22
18-Aug-1995	0.8.10	2	NA-Feb-1998	1.3b4	103
24-Aug-1995	0.8.11	12	19-Feb-1998	1.3b5	3
31-Aug-1995	0.8.12	12	15-Apr-1998	1.3b6	121
07-Sep-1995	0.8.13	11	26-May-1998	1.3b7	84
19-Sep-1995	0.8.14	6	06-Jun-1998	1.3.0	20
14-Oct-1995	0.8.15	22	19-Jul-1998	1.3.1	74
05-Nov-1995	0.8.16	12	23-Sep-1998	1.3.2	90
20-Nov-1995	0.8.17	13	07-Oct-1998	1.3.3	31
23-Nov-1995	1.0.0	1	11-Jan-1999	1.3.4	93
16-Jan-1996	1.0.1	5	22-Mar-1999	1.3.5	69
07-Feb-1999	1.0.2	7	24-Mar-1999	1.3.6	1
16-Feb-1996	1.1b0	1	15-Aug-1999	1.3.7	103
18-Apr-1996	1.0.3	1	18-Aug-1999	1.3.8	12
18-Apr-1996	1.0.4	1	20-Aug-1999	1.3.9	19
20-Apr-1996	1.0.5	1	19-Jan-2000	1.3.10	75
22-Apr-1996	1.1b1	1	21-Jan-2000	1.3.11	1
24-Apr-1996	1.1b2	1	23-Feb-2000	1.3.12	13
10-Jun-1996	1.1b3	14	13-Mar-2000	2.0a1	NA
17-Jun-1996	1.1b4	9	31-Mar-2000	2.0a2	NA
03-Jul-1996	1.1.0	7	30-Apr-2000	2.0a3	NA

Table 1.2: The Apache development efforts

intellectual property and funds on a sound basis, and to provide a vehicle for limiting legal exposure while participating in open-source software projects. Each ASF project is controlled by its own individual project commitee. The Apache HTTP server project is now just one of many ASF projects — although still the most popular one.

Chapter **2**

Apache Functionality

Good design means less design.
Design must serve users,
not try to fool them.

— Dieter Rams,
Chief Designer, Braun

A pache is a very complex web server, mainly because of the vast number of features provided. Fortunately, most of this functionality stays in clearly separated and independent program modules, which facilitates program understanding and maintenance. In this chapter, we look at the Apache program architecture, consisting mainly of a program kernel and various optional modules. We then introduce each module by describing its purpose and the directives that it implements. The order in which modules are presented in this chapter will be repeated again in the other chapters. You can therefore treat this chapter as an overview of the Apache program as a whole and as a departure point from which to examine particular functionalities and implemented directives.

2.1 Apache Architecture

Figure 2.1 on the next page depicts Apache's program architecture. This layering architecture consists of four layers, which are built on top of one another.

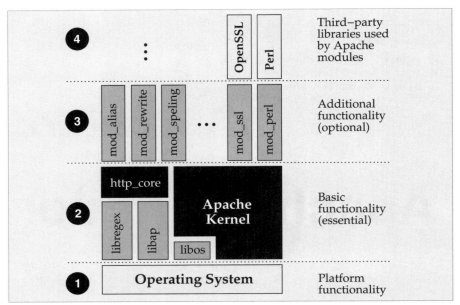

Figure 2.1: The architecture of the Apache web server

❶ **Operating System**
The basic functionality is provided by the underlying operating system. For Apache, this operating system is typically some flavor of UNIX (p.14) , but it can also be Win32, OS/2, MacOS, or even the POSIX subsystems of a mainframe.

❷ **Apache Kernel, Core Module, and Kernel Libraries**
Layer 2 is the main Apache program, consisting of an Apache kernel, a core module, and a few standard libraries. The Apache kernel, together with the special core module (http_core), implements the basic HTTP server functionality and provides the Apache application programming interface (API) to the module layer. This layer also contains a library of generic, reusable code (libap), a library that implements regular expression parsing and matching (libregex), and a small operating system abstraction library (libos).

❸ **Apache Modules**
The impressive user-visible functionality that makes Apache unique among the existing web servers is provided by lots of Apache modules on layer 3. Usually each module implements one clearly separated functionality. In reality, no module is required. Running a minimal web server capable only of serving static documents from a configured

document area is possible even without any modules.[1] This chapter focuses on the standard modules of the Apache program distribution.

❹ **Third-Party Libraries**
For the standard modules (those found in the official Apache distribution), this layer is usually empty.[2] Additional modules, such as mod_ssl and mod_perl, use external third-party libraries, however; these libraries can be found on this layer of the Apache architecture.

The interesting part of this program architecture is the fact that layers 3 and 4 are loosely coupled with layer 2; whereas all modules on layer 3 are designed to remain independent of one another.[3] A side effect of this architecture is that the program code of layers 3 and 4 cannot be statically linked with the program code of layer 1.

In combination with the Dynamic Shared Object (DSO) facility, this structure provides great flexibility. One can therefore assemble the Apache functionality provided by layers 3 and 4 at start-up time (instead of at installation time!) by letting the Apache kernel load the necessary parts.[4]

2.2   Apache Kernel Functionality

The Apache kernel (layer 2 in Figure 2.1 on the facing page) has two purposes: (1) to provide the basic HTTP functionality, and (2) to provide the module API.

▪ **Basic HTTP Server Functionality**
The kernel must support resource handling (through file descriptors, memory segments, and so on), maintain the pre-forked process model, listen to the TCP/IP sockets of the configured virtual servers, transfer control of incoming HTTP requests to the handler processes, handle the HTTP protocol states, and provide read/write buffers, among other duties. Additionally, it provides general functionality like URL and MIME header parsing, DSO loading, and many more capabilities.

▪ **Apache Module API**
As already mentioned, the real functionality of Apache resides inside modules. To allow these modules to fully control the Apache processing, the kernel must provide an API. In Apache, this API consists of a

---

[1] In practice, one at least requires mod_mime.
[2] There might be some exceptions. For instance, some modules need a NDBM library that must usually be provided as an external library when it is not part of the vendor's C library.
[3] Technically, they are not totally independent of one another, because of ordering issues and the shared process address space.
[4] Technically speaking, mod_so loads the DSOs and not the kernel.

static function list in each module (which the kernel uses to dispatch messages between the modules while processing a HTTP request) and a set of API functions (all starting with the common prefix "ap_") that the modules can use. Each HTTP request is divided into ten distinct steps, and each module can hook into each step. At each step, a module can usually either decline or accept to handle the step. To handle the step, the module calls back the kernel through various `ap_xxx()` functions.

For more details about the internals of the Apache API, refer to both the comprehensive documentation inside *Writing Apache Modules with Perl and C* (Lincoln Stein and Doug MacEachern, O'Reilly & Associates Inc., 1999) and the online API documentation under `http://dev.apache.org/apidoc/`.

2.3 Apache Module Functionality

The real user-visible functionality of Apache resides in the various Apache modules. Currently (as of Apache 1.3), the Apache program distribution comes with the core module plus 36 additional standard modules. In this section, we introduce all of these modules plus two important third-party modules: `mod_ssl` and `mod_perl`. Many more third-party modules exist, of course. Each addresses specialized problem situations and solutions. This book, however, covers only the most important modules.

When you need additional functionality, first search for a solution in the *Apache Module Registry* (`http://modules.apache.org/`). The chance is high that you will find a solution there, as more than 140 modules have been registered.

2.3.1 Core Functionality

■ **http_core**   (enabled by default)
Apache Base Functionality
Since Apache 1.0, `src/main/http_core.c`
The Apache Group (1994)

Although the core module http_core uses the Apache Module API, it is not a regular module, because it has hard-coded links and dealings with the kernel.

`http_core` is the base module of Apache, in which all core functionality is implemented. Although this module also uses the Apache Module API, it is a special one: it has a nonstandard file name (`http_core` instead of the expected `mod_core`), it works with special non-API links, and links between the Apache internals and this module are mandatory. In other words, although you can usually strip down Apache at buildtime by removing unnecessary modules, the `http_core` module can never be removed.

Directives:

</**Directory**> ($\rightarrow$ p.71)	**KeepAliveTimeout** ($\rightarrow$ p.81)
</**DirectoryMatch**> ($\rightarrow$ p.71)	**LimitRequestBody** ($\rightarrow$ p.81)
</**Files**> ($\rightarrow$ p.72)	**LimitRequestFields** ($\rightarrow$ p.81)
</**FilesMatch**> ($\rightarrow$ p.72)	**LimitRequestFieldsize** ($\rightarrow$ p.82)
</**IfDefine**> ($\rightarrow$ p.74)	**LimitRequestLine** ($\rightarrow$ p.82)
</**IfModule**> ($\rightarrow$ p.74)	**Listen** ($\rightarrow$ p.83)
</**Limit**> ($\rightarrow$ p.73)	**ListenBacklog** ($\rightarrow$ p.83)
</**Location**> ($\rightarrow$ p.70)	**LockFile** ($\rightarrow$ p.84)
</**LocationMatch**> ($\rightarrow$ p.70)	**LogLevel** ($\rightarrow$ p.84)
</**VirtualHost**> ($\rightarrow$ p.69)	**MaxClients** ($\rightarrow$ p.84)
<**Directory**> ($\rightarrow$ p.71)	**MaxKeepAliveRequests** ($\rightarrow$ p.85)
<**DirectoryMatch**> ($\rightarrow$ p.71)	**MaxRequestsPerChild** ($\rightarrow$ p.85)
<**Files**> ($\rightarrow$ p.72)	**MaxSpareServers** ($\rightarrow$ p.85)
<**FilesMatch**> ($\rightarrow$ p.72)	**MinSpareServers** ($\rightarrow$ p.85)
<**IfDefine**> ($\rightarrow$ p.74)	**NameVirtualHost** ($\rightarrow$ p.86)
<**IfModule**> ($\rightarrow$ p.74)	**Options** ($\rightarrow$ p.86)
<**Limit**> ($\rightarrow$ p.73)	**PidFile** ($\rightarrow$ p.87)
<**Location**> ($\rightarrow$ p.70)	**Port** ($\rightarrow$ p.87)
<**LocationMatch**> ($\rightarrow$ p.70)	**RLimitCPU** ($\rightarrow$ p.87)
<**VirtualHost**> ($\rightarrow$ p.69)	**RLimitMEM** ($\rightarrow$ p.88)
AccessConfig ($\rightarrow$ p.74)	**RLimitNPROC** ($\rightarrow$ p.88)
AccessFileName ($\rightarrow$ p.75)	**Require** ($\rightarrow$ p.89)
AddModule ($\rightarrow$ p.75)	**ResourceConfig** ($\rightarrow$ p.89)
AllowOverride ($\rightarrow$ p.75)	**Satisfy** ($\rightarrow$ p.89)
AuthName ($\rightarrow$ p.76)	**ScoreBoardFile** ($\rightarrow$ p.90)
AuthType ($\rightarrow$ p.76)	**SendBufferSize** ($\rightarrow$ p.90)
BindAddress ($\rightarrow$ p.77)	**ServerAdmin** ($\rightarrow$ p.90)
ClearModuleList ($\rightarrow$ p.77)	**ServerAlias** ($\rightarrow$ p.91)
ContentDigest ($\rightarrow$ p.77)	**ServerName** ($\rightarrow$ p.91)
CoreDumpDirectory ($\rightarrow$ p.78)	**ServerPath** ($\rightarrow$ p.91)
DefaultType ($\rightarrow$ p.78)	**ServerRoot** ($\rightarrow$ p.91)
DocumentRoot ($\rightarrow$ p.78)	**ServerSignature** ($\rightarrow$ p.92)
ErrorDocument ($\rightarrow$ p.78)	**ServerTokens** ($\rightarrow$ p.92)
ErrorLog ($\rightarrow$ p.79)	**ServerType** ($\rightarrow$ p.92)
Group ($\rightarrow$ p.79)	**StartServers** ($\rightarrow$ p.93)
HostnameLookups ($\rightarrow$ p.80)	**Timeout** ($\rightarrow$ p.93)
IdentityCheck ($\rightarrow$ p.80)	**UseCanonicalName** ($\rightarrow$ p.93)
Include ($\rightarrow$ p.80)	**User** ($\rightarrow$ p.94)
KeepAlive ($\rightarrow$ p.81)	

■ **mod_so**   (disabled by default)
Dynamic Shared Object (DSO) Bootstrapping
Since Apache 1.2, `src/modules/standard/mod_so.c`
Robert S. Thau, Alexei Kosut, Paul Sutton, Ralf S. Engelschall (1996)

mod_so is a very interesting module. It supports the DSO facility, which
Apache provides for building modules as stand-alone units (shared object files) and loading them at runtime into the address space of the
httpd process. Thus, although mod_so is implemented as a module, it
provides some bootstrapping functionality for other modules that one
usually would expect to find inside http_core.

mod_so allows you to
load other modules on
demand.

Directives:
> **LoadFile** ($\to$ p.94)   **LoadModule** ($\to$ p.95)

2.3.2   URL Mapping

■ **mod_alias**   (enabled by default)

Simple URL Translation and Redirection
Since Apache 1.0, `src/modules/standard/mod_alias.c`
Rob McCool, David Robinson, Robert S. Thau (1995)

mod_alias is intended for standard URL-to-file name mappings.

`mod_alias` is the father of all URL manipulation modules. It has existed since the early Apache days and provides a limited, but easy-to-understand mechanism for mapping URLs to file names. The original idea was that one could translate URLs to file names by mapping URL prefixes to directory paths on the file system. The `AliasMatch` and `RedirectMatch` directives use regular expressions instead of prefixes to achieve more flexibility.

Directives:
> **Alias** ($\to$ p.95)   **RedirectPermanent** ($\to$ p.97)
> **AliasMatch** ($\to$ p.96)   **RedirectTemp** ($\to$ p.97)
> **Redirect** ($\to$ p.96)   **ScriptAlias** ($\to$ p.97)
> **RedirectMatch** ($\to$ p.96)   **ScriptAliasMatch** ($\to$ p.97)

■ **mod_rewrite**   (disabled by default)

Advanced URL Translation and Redirection
Since Apache 1.2, `src/modules/standard/mod_rewrite.c`
Ralf S. Engelschall (1996)

mod_rewrite is the most powerful URL manipulation solution.

`mod_rewrite` is the Swiss Army Knife of URL manipulations. It provides virtually all of the functions one would ever need to manipulate URLs, and its functionality is highly generalized. Consequently, `mod_rewrite` can be used to solve all sorts of URL-based problems. The drawback is the high learning curve, because this module is based on a complex rule-based matching engine, which uses regular expressions for its patterns. Although the flexibility of `mod_rewrite` makes it a very complex tool, once you understand the basic idea you will master all existing and forthcoming URL-based problems in your webmaster's life.

Directives:
> **RewriteBase** ($\to$ p.100)   **RewriteLogLevel** ($\to$ p.99)
> **RewriteCond** ($\to$ p.100)   **RewriteMap** ($\to$ p.99)
> **RewriteEngine** ($\to$ p.98)   **RewriteOptions** ($\to$ p.98)
> **RewriteLock** ($\to$ p.99)   **RewriteRule** ($\to$ p.101)
> **RewriteLog** ($\to$ p.98)

■ **mod_userdir** (enabled by default)

URL Selection by User Names

Since Apache 1.0, `src/modules/standard/mod_userdir.c`

Rob McCool, Alexei Kosut, Ken Coar (1995)

`mod_userdir` is a module specialized in mapping (/~username) URLs to the home pages of the corresponding users; these home pages are usually found inside the home directory of the user or under one or more dedicated home page areas.

`mod_userdir` finds the home pages of your users.

Directive:

UserDir (→ p.102)

■ **mod_imap** (enabled by default)

URL Selection by Image Map Coordinates

Since Apache 1.0, `src/modules/standard/mod_imap.c`

Rob McCool, Kevin Hughes, Randy Terbush, James H. Cloos, Jr., Nathan Kurz, Mark Cox (1995)

The task of `mod_imap` is simply to determine the surrounding area of x,y-coordinates (given in the `QUERY_STRING`) inside a server-based *image map* and perform an HTTP redirection to the URL corresponding to this area. Although this task is a very specialized one, do not underestimate the difficulty involved in solving this problem. Because image maps can contain arbitrarily complex polygons, a dedicated module to handle this task is only reasonable.

`mod_imap` maps image map coordinates to URLs.

Directives:

ImapBase (→ p.102)   **ImapMenu** (→ p.103)
ImapDefault (→ p.103)

■ **mod_speling** (disabled by default)

URL Spelling Correction

Since Apache 1.3, `src/modules/standard/mod_speling.c`

Alexei Kosut, Martin Kraemer (1997)

`mod_speling` is a very handy module. It corrects minor spelling or capitalization errors in URLs — indeed its droll name provides a hint as to its task. The module addresses this problem by trying to find a matching document, even after all other modules (such as `mod_alias`, `mod_rewrite`, or `mod_userdir`) give up. It works by comparing each document name in the requested directory against the requested document name without regard to case, allowing a maximum of one misspelling (character insertion, omission, transposition, or wrong character). The drawback of this nice feature is that the complicated disk I/O usually increases the response time. Often, it is a better choice to force the user to fix the reference.

`mod_speling` is a nifty URL spell checker that corrects document URLs on-the-fly.

Directive:
  CheckSpelling ($\rightarrow$ p.104)

2.3.3   Access Control

■ **mod_access**   (enabled by default)
Host- and Network-Based Access Control
Since Apache 1.0, `src/modules/standard/mod_access.c`
Rob McCool (1995)

`mod_access`, as its name clearly implies, provides access control for
documents. It allows one to restrict or allow access to resources based
on the client's host name, IP address, or network address. This module
serves as Apache's basic access control mechanism.

mod_access restricts
access through
network identifiers.

Directives:
  Allow ($\rightarrow$ p.104)   **Order** ($\rightarrow$ p.105)
  Deny ($\rightarrow$ p.105)

2.3.4   User Authentication

■ **mod_auth**   (enabled by default)
User Authentication by User Name/Password
Since Apache 1.0, `src/modules/standard/mod_auth.c`
Rob McCool, Robert S. Thau, Dirk van Gulik (1995)

The authentication module `mod_auth` deals with the HTTP Basic Authentication facility, which is simply a user name/password pair sub-
mitted by the client together with the request for a document. This
module allows one to check this information against a flat-file database
similar to UNIX's `/etc/passwd` and `/etc/group` files and to deny access when the given user name/password doesn't match the database
information. Special variants of this module exist that offer the same
functionality but use a database from other than a flat-file (for performance reasons).

mod_auth provides the
HTTP Basic
Authentication facility.

Directives:
  AuthAuthoritative ($\rightarrow$ p.106)   **AuthUserFile** ($\rightarrow$ p.106)
  AuthGroupFile ($\rightarrow$ p.106)

■ **mod_auth_anon**   (disabled by default)
User Authentication by Anonymous Name/E-Mail Address
Since Apache 1.1, `src/modules/standard/mod_auth_anon.c`
Rob McCool, Brian Behlendorf, Robert S. Thau, Dirk van Gulik (1996)

The functionality of mod_auth_anon resembles the behavior of an Anonymous-FTP server, in some ways. That is, this module deals with the Basic Authentication facility like mod_auth. On the other hand, it does not serve any real access control purposes. Instead, it merely identifies the user. One can therefore give the REMOTE_USER variable a meaning in SSI/CGI scripts or log files (for noncritical distinguishing purposes) without requiring real user authentication.

mod_auth_anon
resembles the
Anonymous-FTP idea.

Directives:
Anonymous ($\rightarrow$ p.107)   **Anonymous_MustGiveEmail** ($\rightarrow$ p.108)
Anonymous_Authoritative ($\rightarrow$ p.107)   **Anonymous_NoUserId** ($\rightarrow$ p.108)
Anonymous_LogEmail ($\rightarrow$ p.107)   **Anonymous_VerifyEmail** ($\rightarrow$ p.108)

◼ mod_auth_dbm   (disabled by default)
User Authentication by User Name/Password (UNIX NDBM)
Since Apache 1.0, src/modules/standard/mod_auth_dbm.c
Rob McCool, Robert S. Thau, Dirk van Gulik (1996)

mod_auth_dbm is a variant of mod_auth that provides exactly the same functionality, but uses a standard UNIX NDBM hash file instead of a flat-file database. The advantage is a magnitude-better performance in the lookups (performed for every request) — an especially important consideration when the user community is very large. An NDBM library is provided by most all UNIX platforms.

mod_auth_dbm is the
NDBM-based variant
of mod_auth.

Directives:
AuthDBMAuthoritative ($\rightarrow$ p.108)   **AuthDBMUserFile** ($\rightarrow$ p.109)
AuthDBMGroupFile ($\rightarrow$ p.109)

◼ mod_auth_db   (disabled by default)
User Authentication by User Name/Password (Berkeley-DB)
Since Apache 1.1, src/modules/standard/mod_auth_db.c
Rob McCool, Brian Behlendorf, Robert S. Thau, Andrew Cohen (1996)

mod_auth_db is another variant of mod_auth that provides exactly the same functionality. Instead of a flat-file database, however, it uses a Berkeley-DB/1.x or Berkeley-DB/2.x hash file. The advantage is a magnitude-better performance in the lookups (performed for every request) — an especially important consideration when the user community is very large. The Berkeley-DB library is usually not provided by UNIX platform vendors, but is more reliable and faster than NDBM libraries.

mod_auth_db is the
Berkeley-DB-based
variant of mod_auth.

Directives:
AuthDBAuthoritative ($\rightarrow$ p.110)   **AuthDBUserFile** ($\rightarrow$ p.111)
AuthDBGroupFile ($\rightarrow$ p.110)

■ mod_digest   (disabled by default)
User Authentication by User Name/Realm/Password
Since Apache 1.1, `src/modules/standard/mod_digest.c`
Rob McCool, Robert S. Thau, Alexei Kosut (1996)

mod_digest avoids the transmission of passwords in clear text by using one-way message digests.

In addition to the classical HTTP/1.0 Basic Authentication mechanism, a message digest-based HTTP authentication mechanism exists as defined in RFC 2617.[5] Instead of transferring a clear-text user name/password pair with the HTTP request (which can be easily monitored), a message digest is calculated (via the MD5 algorithm) and transferred together with the user name. This module then performs the same message digest calculation for the password stored in the server's authentication database. When the two digests are equal, access is allowed. This approach offers an obvious advantage relative to Basic Authentication: the password is not sent over the network. The drawback is that many browsers do not support this type of user authentication.

Directive:
AuthDigestFile ($\rightarrow$ p.111)

2.3.5 Content Selection

■ mod_dir   (enabled by default)
Content Selection by Using Directory Default Documents
Since Apache 1.0, `src/modules/standard/mod_dir.c`
Rob McCool, Robert S. Thau (1993)

mod_dir solves the "trailing slash" problem.

mod_dir performs a basic task of any web server: after some URL transformation has mapped a URL to a directory on the local file system, this module tries to select the default document inside this directory. It also solves a related problem: if the URL does not end in a slash (not *xxx/*) but was nevertheless mapped to a directory rather than a file, a slash is appended to the URL and an HTTP redirect is performed to avoid problems with relative hyperlinks inside the document.

Directive:
DirectoryIndex ($\rightarrow$ p.111)

■ mod_actions   (enabled by default)
Content Selection by Content Types and Request Methods
Since Apache 1.1, `src/modules/standard/mod_actions.c`
Alexei Kosut (1996)

---

[5]`ftp://ftp.isi.edu/in-notes/rfc2617.txt`

mod_actions provides a way to trigger a CGI script when a specific MIME content type of a document is encountered or when the request uses a specific HTTP method. This module can be used to create dynamic content when specific documents are requested or to implement special extensional HTTP methods (such as PUT) via CGI scripts.

Directives:
> **Action** (→ p.112)   **Script** (→ p.112)

■ mod_negotiation   (enabled by default)
Content Selection by Best-Matching Client Capabilities
Since Apache 1.0, `src/modules/standard/mod_negotiation.c`
Robert S. Thau, Roy T. Fielding (1995)

The HTTP protocol provides a flexible content negotiation facility controlled by the `Accept` and `Accept-XXX` headers. If `Options MultiViews` is active, the `mod_negotiation` module chooses the best representation of a resource (when a resource is available in several different representations, of course) based on the client-supplied preferences for media type, languages, character set, and encoding. It also implements features intended to provide more intelligent handling of requests for clients that send incomplete negotiation information. The internal algorithms in this module are very complex and partly even heuristic, which makes this module really nontrivial — both to understand and to use.

> `mod_negotiation` provides complex content negotiations.

Directives:
> **CacheNegotiatedDocs** (→ p.113)   **LanguagePriority** (→ p.113)

2.3.6   Environment Creation

■ mod_env   (enabled by default)
Fixed Environment Variable Creation
Since Apache 1.1, `src/modules/standard/mod_env.c`
Andrew Wilson (1995)

mod_env is a very simple module that performs one basic task: it controls the export of variables to the SSI/CGI environment and allows the webmaster to force values of variables.

> `mod_env` controls the CGI environment.

Directives:
> **PassEnv** (→ p.114)   **UnsetEnv** (→ p.114)
> **SetEnv** (→ p.114)

■ **mod_setenvif**   (enabled by default)

Conditional Environment Variable Creation

Since Apache 1.2, `src/modules/standard/mod_setenvif.c`

Alexei Kosut, Paul Sutton (1996)

`mod_setenvif` is a more advanced module for setting SSI/CGI environment variables. It sets variables depending on various client information found in the HTTP request. This ability is useful when combined with a special variable-based feature of the core module's `deny` and `allow` directives. In addition, some internal HTTP protocol behaviors of Apache can be controlled through variables that are usually set with the `SetEnvIf` directive of this module.

> `mod_setenvif` conditionally sets environment variables.

Directives:

BrowserMatch ($\rightarrow$ p.114)	**SetEnvIf** ($\rightarrow$ p.115)
BrowserMatchNoCase ($\rightarrow$ p.115)	**SetEnvIfNoCase** ($\rightarrow$ p.116)

■ **mod_unique_id**   (disabled by default)

Generation of Unique Identifiers by Request

Since Apache 1.3, `src/modules/standard/mod_unique_id.c`

Dean Gaudet, Alvaro Martinez Echevarria (1997)

`mod_unique_id` performs a simple but sometimes useful task: it generates a magic token for each HTTP request that is guaranteed to be unique across *all* requests under very specific conditions. The identifier will even be unique across multiple machines in a properly configured cluster of machines. It is exported to the SSI/CGI environment as a variable.

> `mod_unique_id` generates unique identifiers for each request.

Directives: *none*

2.3.7 Server-Side Scripting

■ **mod_cgi**   (enabled by default)

Common Gateway Interface (CGI) Implementation

Since Apache 1.0, `src/modules/standard/mod_cgi.c`

Rob McCool, Robert S. Thau (1995)

The *Common Gateway Interface* (CGI) is the classical interface for generating dynamic content on the web. It is basically a set of environment variables that the server provides to a program while spawning a specific request to create the dynamic content. CGI remains the only truly portable and standardized scripting environment provided by web servers. Unfortunately, this way of creating dynamic content requires many resources (spawning a subprocess costs many extra memory and CPU cycles) and increases the response time. Alternative solutions are possible, for instance, with `mod_perl`.

> `mod_cgi` provides the Common Gateway Interface.

Directives:
    ScriptLog ($\rightarrow$ p.116)   **ScriptLogLength** ($\rightarrow$ p.117)
    ScriptLogBuffer ($\rightarrow$ p.117)

▪ mod_include   (enabled by default)

Server-Side Includes (SSI) Implementation
Since Apache 1.0, `src/modules/standard/mod_include.c`
The Apache Group (1995)

`mod_include` implements an extended version of the *Server-Side Includes* (SSI) quasi-standard, (which was originally introduced by the NCSA httpd). Embedded programming constructs in an HTML document are evaluated "on the fly" and expanded by the server before the document is sent to the client. The name of the module relates to a major goal of SSI — its role as a file inclusion facility — but please note that using this facility decreases server performance.

> `mod_include` provides Server-Side Includes.

Directive:
    XBitHack ($\rightarrow$ p.117)

2.3.8   Response Header Generation

▪ mod_mime   (enabled by default)

Fixed Content Type/Encoding Assignment
Since Apache 1.0, `src/modules/standard/mod_mime.c`
Rob McCool (1995)

`mod_mime` provides for static assigning of MIME content types and content encodings to documents. This assignment is primarily carried out through the file extensions of the documents. For more advanced mappings, one can use `mod_mime_magic`. Nevertheless, `mod_mime` is very important in Apache, because many other modules depend on `mod_mime` content-type tables.

> `mod_mime` assigns MIME types to documents.

Directives:
    AddEncoding ($\rightarrow$ p.118)   **ForceType** ($\rightarrow$ p.119)
    AddHandler ($\rightarrow$ p.118)   **RemoveHandler** ($\rightarrow$ p.120)
    AddLanguage ($\rightarrow$ p.118)   **SetHandler** ($\rightarrow$ p.120)
    AddType ($\rightarrow$ p.119)   **TypesConfig** ($\rightarrow$ p.120)
    DefaultLanguage ($\rightarrow$ p.119)

▪ mod_mime_magic   (disabled by default)

Automatic Content Type/Encoding Assignment
Since Apache 1.3, `src/modules/standard/mod_mime_magic.c`
Ian F. Darwin, Ian Kluft (1997)

mod_mime_magic provides for dynamic assignment of MIME content types and encodings to documents. In contrast to mod_mime, this module looks directly at the content of the document (usually its first bytes) and tries to guess the content type and encoding by matching so-called magic cookies (byte sequences that are unique to particular file formats). The resulting performance penalty should not be neglected. Thus, it is a good idea to manually define as many commonly known and straight forward MIME-types as possible with mod_mime, so mod_mime_magic has to determine only the remaining ones.

mod_mime_magic is a nifty variant of mod_mime that guesses MIME types by inspecting the first bytes of a document.

Directive:

MimeMagicFile ($\rightarrow$ p.121)

■ mod_expires (disabled by default)
Creation of HTTP Expires Header
Since Apache 1.2, src/modules/standard/mod_expires.c
Andrew Wilson (1996)

mod_expire provides and controls the HTTP Expires header field.

mod_expires controls the setting of the HTTP Expires header field in server responses. The expiration date can be set relative to either the time of the source document's last modification, or the time of the last client access. This information informs the client and intermediate HTTP proxies about the document's validity and persistence. If cached, the document may be fetched from the cache rather than from the source until the expiration date has passed. After that time, the cache copy is considered "expired" and invalid, and a new copy must be obtained from the source.

Directives:
ExpiresActive ($\rightarrow$ p.121)   **ExpiresDefault** ($\rightarrow$ p.122)
ExpiresByType ($\rightarrow$ p.121)

■ mod_headers (disabled by default)
Creation of Arbitrary HTTP Headers
Since Apache 1.2, src/modules/standard/mod_headers.c
Paul Sutton (1996)

mod_headers allows you to set arbitrary HTTP response header fields.

mod_headers can add arbitrary HTTP header fields in the server response. Any header field can be replaced, deleted, or extended. It therefore allows you to tailor arbitrary HTTP responses.

Directive:

Header ($\rightarrow$ p.122)

■ mod_cern_meta (disabled by default)
Creation of Arbitrary HTTP Headers (CERN-style)
Since Apache 1.1, src/modules/standard/mod_cern_meta.c
Andrew Wilson (1996)

mod_cern_meta is a backward-compatible module that provides approximately the same functionality as mod_headers, albeit in a some-
what different way. Instead of being configured through Apache directives, the headers are placed inside a dedicated *meta*-file.

mod_cern_meta is a
variant of mod_headers
that uses external files.

Directives:
   MetaDir ($\rightarrow$ p.123)   **MetaSuffix** ($\rightarrow$ p.123)
   MetaFiles ($\rightarrow$ p.123)

2.3.9   Internal Content Handlers

■ **mod_asis**   (enabled by default)
Generation of Raw Responses
Since Apache 1.0, src/modules/standard/mod_asis.c
The Apache Group (1995)

mod_asis allows file types to be defined so that Apache will send them
as is, without adding HTTP headers. It can be used to send any kind
of data from the server, including redirects and other special HTTP
responses, without the use of a CGI program.

mod_asis allows you to
send out arbitrary
HTTP responses.

Directives: *none*

■ **mod_autoindex**   (enabled by default)
Generation of Directory Index Documents
Since Apache 1.0, src/modules/standard/mod_autoindex.c
Rob McCool, Robert S. Thau (1993)

The index document of a directory (requested with a URL ending in a
slash) can come from one of two sources: a file written by the user or a
listing generated by the server. This module uses the latter source. The
layout of such on-the-fly generated index listings can be controlled in
many different ways.

mod_autoindex is
Apache's built-in "ls
-l" function.

Directives:
   AddAlt ($\rightarrow$ p.124)   **DefaultIcon** ($\rightarrow$ p.126)
   AddAltByEncoding ($\rightarrow$ p.124)   **FancyIndexing** ($\rightarrow$ p.126)
   AddAltByType ($\rightarrow$ p.125)   **HeaderName** ($\rightarrow$ p.127)
   AddDescription ($\rightarrow$ p.125)   **IndexIgnore** ($\rightarrow$ p.127)
   AddIcon ($\rightarrow$ p.125)   **IndexOptions** ($\rightarrow$ p.127)
   AddIconByEncoding ($\rightarrow$ p.126) **IndexOrderDefault** ($\rightarrow$ p.128)
   AddIconByType ($\rightarrow$ p.126)   **ReadmeName** ($\rightarrow$ p.128)

■ **mod_status**   (enabled by default)
Display Summary of Server Runtime Information
Since Apache 1.1, src/modules/standard/mod_status.c
Mark Cox (1995)

mod_status provides a content handler that can be mapped to a URL
and that outputs a runtime status page when requested. In particular,

internal process information is displayed. A variant can be displayed that gives a simple machine-readable list of the current server state. Always think about your privacy before using this module.

Directive:

ExtendedStatus ($\rightarrow$ p.129)

▓ mod_info   (disabled by default)
Display Summary of Server Configuration-Time Information
Since Apache 1.1, `src/modules/standard/mod_info.c`
Rasmus Lerdorf, Lou Langholtz (1996)

mod_info provides a content handler that can be mapped to a URL and that outputs a configuration-time information page when requested. This page includes the compiled-in modules and all configuration directives that are present in the server configuration files.

> mod_info shamelessly publishes your server configuration.

Directive:

AddModuleInfo ($\rightarrow$ p.129)

2.3.10   Request Logging

▓ mod_log_config   (enabled by default)
Generic Request Logging
Since Apache 1.0, `src/modules/standard/mod_log_config.c`
Robert S. Thau (1995)

mod_log_config provides for logging of the requests made to the web server, using the *Common Log Format* (CLF) or any other user-specified format. It uses `printf(3)`-style format strings to define the log file entries. These entries can be written to a file or a reliable pipe connected to a spawned program.

> mod_log_config allows the writing of custom log files.

Directives:

CookieLog ($\rightarrow$ p.129)	**LogFormat** ($\rightarrow$ p.130)
CustomLog ($\rightarrow$ p.130)	**TransferLog** ($\rightarrow$ p.130)

▓ mod_log_agent   (disabled by default)
Specialized User-Agent Logging (Deprecated)
Since Apache 1.0, `src/modules/standard/mod_log_agent.c`
The Apache Group (1995)

mod_log_agent is deprecated because it has been superseded by mod_log_config. It provides logging of the User-Agent HTTP header information.

Directive:
> **AgentLog** ($\to$ p.131)

▪ mod_log_referer (disabled by default)
Specialized Referrer Logging (Deprecated)
Since Apache 1.0, `src/modules/standard/mod_log_referer.c`
The Apache Group (1995)

`mod_log_referer` is deprecated because it has been superseded by `mod_log_config`. It provides logging of the `Referer` HTTP header information.

Directives:
> **RefererIgnore** ($\to$ p.131)   **RefererLog** ($\to$ p.131)

▪ mod_usertrack (disabled by default)
Specialized User Click-Trail Logging
Since Apache 1.0, `src/modules/standard/mod_usertrack.c`
Mark J. Cox (1995)

`mod_usertrack` is a module that implements a nifty idea, but that suffers from nasty side effects in practice. It generates a *clickstream* log of user activity on the server by using HTTP *cookies* (information included by the server in responses that is stored by the client and sent back to the server on subsequent requests). Unfortunately, not all clients support cookies. In addition, many clients, by default, require an interactive user dialog to accept cookies. The use of HTTP cookies defeats caching, too. These facts make the theoretically useful facility mostly unusable in practice.

> `mod_usertrack` tracks user activity via HTTP cookies.

Directives:
> **CookieExpires** ($\to$ p.132)   **CookieTracking** ($\to$ p.132)
> **CookieName** ($\to$ p.132)

2.3.11 Experimental

▪ mod_mmap_static (disabled by default)
Caching of Frequently Served Pages via Memory Mapping
Since Apache 1.3, `src/modules/experimental/mod_mmap_static.c`
Dean Gaudet (1997)

Serving static pages from disk is the main task of a web server. The `mod_mmap_static` module maps a statically configured list of frequently requested (but not changed) documents into memory by using the UNIX `mmap(2)` function. Although this approach can dramatically reduce the response time and I/O consumption, it unfortunately brings nasty

> `mod_mmap_static` is experimental and memory-maps documents for fastest serving.

problems: every time a file changes, a reload of the server is required to remap the new contents into memory because mmap(2) doesn't allow automatic refreshments.

Directive:
MMapFile ($\rightarrow$ p.133)

■ **mod_example** (disabled by default)
Apache API Demonstration (Developers Only)
Since Apache 1.2, src/modules/example/mod_example.c
Ken Coar (1997)

mod_example is a demonstration-only module. It allows Apache module authors to easily explore the Apache Module API. The module basically hooks into every API processing phase, enabling developers to observe the API processing steps. It should never be used within a production server, of course.

> mod_example lets developers learn the internal processing stages of the Apache API.

Directive:
Example ($\rightarrow$ p.133)

2.3.12 Extensional Functionality

■ **mod_proxy** (disabled by default)
Caching Proxy Implementation for HTTP and FTP
Since Apache 1.1, src/modules/proxy/mod_proxy.c
Ben Laurie, Chuck Murcko (1996)

> mod_proxy is one of the stepchild modules of Apache.

mod_proxy implements a caching proxy inside Apache. This proxy facility can be used either as a real web proxy by the clients or as a back end by other modules (such as mod_rewrite) for performing HTTP client tasks. Although this module opens the door to a lot of nifty solutions, it currently remains a "stepchild" inside Apache. It was designed when HTTP/1.0 was considered state of the art. With HTTP/1.1, however, the requirements for a proxy changed dramatically. Also, with the initial design one could not provide real HTTP/1.1-conforming proxy functionality. Thus, although Apache (as an origin server) is fully HTTP/1.1 compliant, the proxy module is just HTTP/1.0 compliant. Whereas this module is no longer used to establish a real proxy server, it remains of interest when applied in conjunction with other modules like mod_rewrite or mod_ssl.

Directives:

AllowCONNECT (→ p.134)	**NoCache** (→ p.137)
CacheDefaultExpire (→ p.138)	**NoProxy** (→ p.134)
CacheDirLength (→ p.138)	**ProxyBlock** (→ p.135)
CacheDirLevels (→ p.138)	**ProxyDomain** (→ p.135)
CacheForceCompletion (→ p.140)	**ProxyPass** (→ p.136)
CacheGcInterval (→ p.139)	**ProxyPassReverse** (→ p.137)
CacheLastModifiedFactor (→ p.139)	**ProxyReceiveBufferSize** (→ p.136)
CacheMaxExpire (→ p.139)	**ProxyRemote** (→ p.135)
CacheRoot (→ p.137)	**ProxyRequests** (→ p.134)
CacheSize (→ p.138)	**ProxyVia** (→ p.136)

■ **mod_perl**   (disabled by default)

Perl Integration and Interface
Since Apache 1.1, src/modules/perl/mod_perl.c (third-party)
Doug MacEachern (1996)

The mod_perl third-party module integrates the Perl programming language into the Apache web server by providing the Apache Module API (written in ANSI C) at the Perl programming level. One can therefore easily extend the Apache web server by writing extensions in Perl, which is a much easier task than writing an Apache module in ANSI C. Many interesting Perl modules for Apache (usually named Apache::-XXX) already exist and provide high-level features for Apache. One of the most interesting standard use cases for mod_perl is Apache::Registry: In an alternative CGI implementation, the CGI scripts (written in Perl) are precompiled into byte-code, cached, and on request executed inside the address space of the Apache process. With this approach, the response time is a magnitude faster and the resource requirements are reduced.

mod_perl combines the flexibility of Apache with the programming power of Perl.

Directives:

</Perl> (→ p.141)	**PerlLogHandler** (→ p.148)
<Perl> (→ p.141)	**PerlModule** (→ p.143)
=cut (→ p.141)	**PerlOpmask** (→ p.143)
=pod (→ p.141)	**PerlPassEnv** (→ p.144)
PerlAccessHandler (→ p.147)	**PerlPostReadRequestHandler** (→ p.146)
PerlAuthenHandler (→ p.147)	**PerlRequire** (→ p.143)
PerlAuthzHandler (→ p.147)	**PerlRestartHandler** (→ p.150)
PerlChildExitHandler (→ p.149)	**PerlSendHeader** (→ p.145)
PerlChildInitHandler (→ p.145)	**PerlSetEnv** (→ p.144)
PerlCleanupHandler (→ p.149)	**PerlSetVar** (→ p.144)
PerlDispatchHandler (→ p.149)	**PerlSetupEnv** (→ p.144)
PerlFixupHandler (→ p.148)	**PerlTaintCheck** (→ p.142)
PerlFreshRestart (→ p.142)	**PerlTransHandler** (→ p.146)
PerlHandler (→ p.148)	**PerlTypeHandler** (→ p.147)
PerlHeaderParserHandler (→ p.146)	**PerlWarn** (→ p.142)
PerlInitHandler (→ p.145)	**__END__** (→ p.141)

■ **mod_ssl**   (disabled by default)
SSL/TLS Integration and Interface
Since Apache 1.3, `src/modules/ssl/mod_ssl.c` (third-party)
Ralf S. Engelschall (1998)

mod_ssl combines the
flexibility of Apache
with the security of
OpenSSL.

The mod_ssl third-party module provides strong cryptography via the *Secure Sockets Layer* (SSL version 2/3) and *Transport Layer Security* (TLS version 1) protocols with the help of the SSL/TLS implementation toolkit OpenSSL. SSL/TLS is a generic cryptography protocol that resides on top of TCP/IP (but below protocols like HTTP) and is used inside web servers to provide the HTTPS protocol (which mainly is HTTP over SSL/TLS over TCP/IP). The mod_ssl module here forms the essential glue code between the OpenSSL toolkit and the Apache web server.

Directives:

SSLCACertificateFile ($\rightarrow$ p.154)	**SSLOptions** ($\rightarrow$ p.157)
SSLCACertificatePath ($\rightarrow$ p.154)	**SSLPassPhraseDialog** ($\rightarrow$ p.150)
SSLCARevocationFile ($\rightarrow$ p.155)	**SSLProtocol** ($\rightarrow$ p.152)
SSLCARevocationPath ($\rightarrow$ p.154)	**SSLRandomSeed** ($\rightarrow$ p.151)
SSLCertificateFile ($\rightarrow$ p.153)	**SSLRequire** ($\rightarrow$ p.158)
SSLCertificateKeyFile ($\rightarrow$ p.153)	**SSLRequireSSL** ($\rightarrow$ p.157)
SSLCipherSuite ($\rightarrow$ p.152)	**SSLSessionCache** ($\rightarrow$ p.151)
SSLEngine ($\rightarrow$ p.152)	**SSLSessionCacheTimeout** ($\rightarrow$ p.152)
SSLLog ($\rightarrow$ p.156)	**SSLVerifyClient** ($\rightarrow$ p.155)
SSLLogLevel ($\rightarrow$ p.156)	**SSLVerifyClientDepth** ($\rightarrow$ p.155)
SSLMutex ($\rightarrow$ p.150)	

Chapter **3**

Building Apache

*The software said it requires Microsoft
IIS 4 or better, so I installed Apache.*

— Unknown (paraphrased)

In this chapter, we first discuss the process of building a full-featured Apache web server with Perl scripting and SSL/TLS capabilities; our discussion takes the form of a step-by-step tutorial that introduces the *Apache AutoConf-style Interface* (APACI). The procedure includes getting and extracting the distributions, configuring the source trees, building the packages, and finally installing the packages. A complete reference follows the tutorial and covers all command-line variables and options of APACI in detail. Selected Apache configuration special topics are also discussed in more detail at the end of the chapter.

3.1   Sample Step-by-Step Installation

In the first part of this chapter, we show a complete step-by-step installation procedure for an Apache server including two extensions, `mod_perl` and `mod_ssl`. These two particular modules were selected because they are also covered in Chapter 4 (the configuration chapter). Other popular third-party modules such as `mod_php3`, `mod_dav`, and `mod_jserv` can be added in an analogous fashion. You can therefore treat this section as an installation tutorial

Here we build a
full-featured Apache
web server with Perl
scripting and SSL/TLS
capabilities.

intended to help you better understand the configuration reference in Section 3.2 and to get a general impression of how to perform a complex Apache installation.

3.1.1 File System Preparation

As the first step, you must decide where the server package should be installed. That is, you have to choose a common installation path prefix, such as `/usr/local/apache`. This prefix is important because it is required repeatedly in the installation procedure. All packages will be installed in subdirectories under this prefix. The file system on which this path prefix will reside must have at least 25MB of free disk space available. In addition, you need a working directory where the packages can be built prior to the installation. For this temporary area, additional disk space of at least 60MB is required.

For installing Apache you need 25MB free disk space for installation plus 60MB temporary disk space.

3.1.2 Obtaining the Source Distribution

Next, you must obtain the Apache source distribution. Although so-called binary distributions are available, we recommend that you start with the source distribution, except in those very rare cases where no C compiler is available. First, determine the latest version number of Apache by looking at the Apache home page (`http://www.apache.org/httpd`). It always includes a note about the latest version.

Package	Source Distribution
Apache	`http://www.apache.org/dist/apache_1.3.12.tar.gz`
mod_perl	`http://perl.apache.org/src/mod_perl-1.24.tar.gz`
Perl	`http://www.perl.com/cpan/src/5.0/perl-5.005_03.tar.gz`
mod_ssl	`http://www.modssl.org/source/mod_ssl-2.6.6-1.3.12.tar.gz`
OpenSSL	`http://www.openssl.org/source/openssl-0.9.6.tar.gz`

Table 3.1: The involved software packages

For instance, at the time of this writing, the most recent Apache version was 1.3.12. To grab the source distribution, you can use a browser and fetch it via HTTP from the area `http://www.apache.org/dist/`. Apache is also available from mirror locations around the world. The list of available locations can be found at `http://www.apache.org/mirrors/`.

All of these software packages are available free of charge on the Internet.

In this book, we also cover two popular Apache extensions, mod_perl (the Apache interface to Perl) and mod_ssl (the Apache interface to OpenSSL). You must therefore obtain the distributions of four additional packages: the Perl interpreter (`www.perl.com`), the mod_perl module (`perl.apache.org`), the OpenSSL toolkit (`www.openssl.org`), and the `mod_ssl` module (`www.mod-ssl.org`).

Table 3.1 on the preceding page summarizes the download locations for the latest stable version of all involved packages. If they have changed since this book's publication, start over with the home page of the package to find the latest version and current download location.

To build the packages, move the distribution files into your chosen working directory and extract the five distribution "tarballs" there.

```
$  gunzip -c apache_1.3.12.tar.gz | tar xvf -
apache_1.3.12/
apache_1.3.12/src/
apache_1.3.12/src/ap/
  :

$  gunzip -c mod_perl-1.24.tar.gz | tar xvf -
mod_perl-1.24/
mod_perl-1.24/t/
mod_perl-1.24/t/docs/
  :

$  gunzip -c perl-5.005_03.tar.gz | tar xvf -
perl5.005_03/
perl5.005_03/Artistic
perl5.005_03/Changes
  :

$  gunzip -c mod_ssl-2.6.6-1.3.12.tar.gz | tar xvf -
mod_ssl-2.6.6-1.3.12/ANNOUNCE
mod_ssl-2.6.6-1.3.12/CHANGES
mod_ssl-2.6.6-1.3.12/CREDITS
  :

$  gunzip -c openssl-0.9.6.tar.gz | tar xvf -
openssl-0.9.6/CHANGES
openssl-0.9.6/CHANGES.SSLeay
openssl-0.9.6/Configure
  :
```

3.1.3 Package Prerequisites

The Apache build process discussed later in this chapter depends on the availability of the `mod_perl` and `mod_ssl` modules. But these, in turn, depend on the Perl and OpenSSL third-party packages. For this reason, a prerequisite to building Apache with these modules is to build these two packages first. Follow these steps to install Perl and OpenSSL:

> To build the complex Apache modules, the third-party packages must usually be installed first.

- ■ Go into the source tree of Perl and follow the directions in the `INSTALL` document found there. The typical installation steps will look like the following:

```
$  cd perl-5.005_03

$  sh Configure -d -s -e -Dprefix=/usr/local/apache
First let's make sure your kit is complete.  Checking...
Locating common programs...
   :
$  make
'sh cflags libperl.a miniperlmain.o'  miniperlmain.c
   CCCMD = cc -DPERL_CORE -c -I/usr/local/include -O
   :
$  make install
./perl installperl
mkdir /usr/local/apache/bin
   :
$  (cd /usr/include; /usr/local/apache/bin/h2ph *.h sys/*.h machine/*.h)
a.out.h -> a.out.ph
acl.h -> acl.ph
   :
$  cd ..
```

■ Go into the source tree of OpenSSL and follow the directions in its
   INSTALL document. The typical installation steps will be similar to the
   following:

Good packages
usually do not require
you to manually edit
their configuration.
Instead, they provide
some sort of
autoconfiguration
mechanism.

```
$  cd openssl-0.9.6

$  sh config --prefix=/usr/local/apache
Operating system: i386-whatever-freebsd3
Configuring for FreeBSD-elf
   :
$  make
making all in crypto...
echo "#define DATE "'date'" >date.h
gcc -I. -I../include -DTERMIOS -DL_ENDIAN ...
   :
$  make install
installing crypto...
making install in crypto/md2...
   :
$  cd ..
```

After you complete these steps, the Perl interpreter and the OpenSSL toolkit
will be installed under /usr/local/apache. Now, you must proceed with
the application of mod_perl and mod_ssl to the Apache source tree.

Complex Apache
modules usually
provide automated
ways to get to the
Apache source tree.
Most rely on APACI
features.

Follow these steps:

■ Go into the source tree of mod_perl and follow the directions in the
   INSTALL.apaci document found there. Many configuration options
   are available for mod_perl, although the typical installation steps will
   look like the following:

$ *cd mod_perl-1.24*

$ */usr/local/apache/bin/perl Makefile.PL APACHE_SRC=../apache_1.3.12*

 DO_HTTPD=1 USE_APACI=1 PREP_HTTPD=1 EVERYTHING=1

```
Will configure via APACI
(cd ../apache_1.3.12/src && ./Configure -file Configuration)
```
 ⋮

$ *make*

```
mkdir blib
mkdir blib/lib
cp ../apache_1.3.12/src/include/http_protocol.h ...
```
 ⋮

$ *make install*

```
Installing /usr/local/apache/lib/perl5/site_perl/5.005/...
```
 ⋮

$ *cd ..*

■ Go into the source tree of `mod_ssl` and follow the directions in its `INST-ALL` document. Once again, many configuration options are available, but the typical installation steps will look like the following:

$ *cd mod_ssl-2.6.6-1.3.12*

$ *./configure --with-apache=../apache_1.3.12*

```
Configuring mod_ssl/2.6.3 for Apache/1.3.12
+ Apache location: ../apache_1.3.12 (Version 1.3.12)
```
 ⋮

$ *cd ..*

3.1.4   Configuring the Apache Source Tree

The next major step is to configure the Apache source tree. You must select the desired modules, the compiler and flags used for building, the installation path layout, and other features. Typically, you will use the *Apache AutoConf-style Interface* (APACI) — a script named "`configure`" you will find in the top-level of the Apache source tree.[1] This script provides numerous options that allow you to flexibly configure the build and installation. A complete option reference appears in Section 3.2.

The recommended standard way to configure the Apache 1.3 source tree is the new Apache AutoConf-style Interface.

The minimal configuration step usually takes the following form:

$ *cd apache_1.3.12*

$ *./configure --prefix=/usr/local/apache*

---

[1] In the configuration method of Apache 1.2, you had to manually edit a configuration file (`src/Configuration`) and run the script (`src/Configure`) on it. Because this older facility doesn't provide installation support, you are strongly advised to use APACI unless you are an Apache expert. Even when you are an Apache expert, you'll discover that these editing steps can be carried out via APACI's command-line options as well.

```
Configuring for Apache, Version 1.3.12
  :
$  cd ..
```

Because we want to build Apache with our two additional modules and because it's reasonable to build Apache as flexibly as possible with the help of the *Dynamic Shared Object* (DSO) facility, we recommend the following steps:

APACI offers lots of command-line options, which at first look are ugly. Once you become familiar with APACI, you will enjoy its consistent and batch-capable nature.

$ *cd apache_1.3.12*

$ *env SSL_BASE=/usr/local/apache ./configure*

  --target=apache

  --with-layout=GNU

  --without-confadjust

  --prefix=/usr/local/apache

  --with-perl=/usr/local/apache/bin/perl

  --activate-module=src/modules/perl/libperl.a

  --enable-module=perl

  --enable-module=ssl

  --enable-shared=remain

```
Configuring for Apache, Version 1.3.12
 + using installation path layout: GNU (config.layout)
 + activated perl module (modules/perl/libperl.a)
Creating Makefile
Creating Configuration.apaci in src
Creating Makefile in src
 + configured for FreeBSD 3.1 platform
 + setting C compiler to gcc
 + setting C pre-processor to gcc -E
 + checking for system header files
 + using custom target name: apache
 + adding selected modules
    o rewrite_module uses ConfigStart/End
      enabling DBM support for mod_rewrite
    o dbm_auth_module uses ConfigStart/End
    o db_auth_module uses ConfigStart/End
      using Berkeley-DB/1.x for mod_auth_db (-lc)
    o ssl_module uses ConfigStart/End
      + SSL interface: mod_ssl/2.6.3
      + SSL interface build type: OBJ
      + SSL interface compatibility: enabled
      + SSL interface experimental code: disabled
      + SSL interface vendor extensions: disabled
      + SSL interface plugin: Vendor DBM (libc)
      + SSL library path: /usr/local/apache
      + SSL library version: OpenSSL 0.9.6
      + SSL library type: installed package (stand-alone)
      + SSL library plugin mode: none
```

```
    o perl_module uses ConfigStart/End
      + mod_perl build type: OBJ
      + id: mod_perl/1.24
      + id: Perl/5.00503 (freebsd) [/usr/local/apache/bin/perl]
      + setting up mod_perl build environment
      + adjusting Apache build environment
      + enabling Perl support for SSI (mod_include)
  + enabling Extended API (EAPI)
  + doing sanity check on compiler and options
Creating Makefile in src/support
  :
```

These steps configure Apache as follows:

APACI options are just what their name implies: optional. Don't get confused by the large number of available options – they are just available for fine-tuning, but are not mandatory.

1. The SSL_BASE variable locates the installed OpenSSL package for module mod_ssl.

2. --target names the program "apache" (the default is "httpd").

3. --with-layout selects a GNU-style file system layout (the default is an old-style "Apache" layout).

4. --prefix specifies the installation path prefix.

5. --sbindir ensures that all binaries are installed into a single directory for binaries.

6. --with-perl locates the installed Perl package for mod_perl.

7. --activate-module activates the mod_perl module for the configuration process.

8. The two --enable-module options enable mod_perl and mod_ssl.

9. --enable-shared forces all unenabled modules to be built as DSOs for later loading on demand.

3.1.5   Building and Installing Apache

The final step is to actually build the Apache package ingredients and install them under our selected installation path prefix. Because we used APACI, this task is easy and usually involves only two simple commands:

```
$ make
===> src
===> src/os/unix
gcc -c -I../..  -I../../os/unix -I../../ ...
  :
$ make install
===> [mktree: Creating Apache installation tree]
./src/helpers/mkdir.sh /usr/local/apache/bin
./src/helpers/mkdir.sh /usr/local/apache/bin
  :
```

Of course, we used `mod_ssl`. Consequently, a X.509 server certificate and private key are required, though they can be dummy ones for testing purposes. The following steps are required in our situation:

```
$ make
===> src
===> src/os/unix
gcc -c -I../..  -I../../os/unix -I../../ ...
    :
$ make certificate TYPE=dummy
SSL Certificate Generation Utility (mkcert.sh)
    :
$ make install
===> [mktree: Creating Apache installation tree]
./src/helpers/mkdir.sh /usr/local/apache/bin
./src/helpers/mkdir.sh /usr/local/apache/bin
    :
```

Installing a ready-to-run Apache web server with the help of APACI is just a matter of a few make commands.

Voilà! You have now successfully installed an Apache web server including `mod_perl` and `mod_ssl` under /usr/local/apache. Your reward is an out-of-the-box usable Apache web server including Perl scripting and SSL/TLS functionality. To verify that it works properly, fire up your new server from the root user account . . .

```
$ su
Password:
# /usr/local/apache/sbin/apachectl startssl
/usr/local/apache/bin/apachectl startssl: httpd started
% $ ps -ax | grep -i apache
% 8593  ??  Ss     0:01.87 /usr/local/apache/sbin/apache -DSSL
% 8594  ??  S      0:00.00 /usr/local/apache/sbin/apache -DSSL
% 8595  ??  S      0:00.00 /usr/local/apache/sbin/apache -DSSL
% 8596  ??  S      0:00.00 /usr/local/apache/sbin/apache -DSSL
% 8597  ??  S      0:00.00 /usr/local/apache/sbin/apache -DSSL
% 8598  ??  S      0:00.00 /usr/local/apache/sbin/apache -DSSL
```

. . . and try to connect to it with your favorite browser via both HTTP and HTTPS through the URLs `http://localhost/` and `https://localhost/`. Both protocols should be usable.

3.2 Configuration Reference

The following is a complete reference to the APACI command line. The various APACI command-line variables and options enable you to adjust the way Apache is built and installed. The command line has the following general structure:

```
$ env [VARIABLE=value ...] ./configure [--option=value ...]
```

3.2.1 Configuration Variables

The following *VARIABLE*s are taken from the APACI environment:

- ### CC
C Compiler Program

    Example: `CC="egcc"`

    Specifies the C compiler program to use when building the Apache object files and executables. The default is platform-dependent — Apache selects the best choice when more than one compiler is installed on the platform. You can also use this variable to force the usage of a particular compiler, however.

- ### CFLAGS
C Compiler Standard Flags

    Example: `CFLAGS="-Wall -pendantic"`

    Specifies standard flags for the C compiler. These flags will be used on the `CC` command lines. The exception is "`-I`", which (for historical reasons) should be specified with `INCLUDES`.

- ### OPTIM
C Compiler Optimization Flags

    Example: `OPTIM="-pipe -O2"`

    Specifies the C compiler optimization flags. These flags can also be specified via `CFLAGS`, but for historical reasons they have their own variable.

- ### INCLUDES
C Compiler Include Flags

    Example: `INCLUDES="-I/usr/local/include"`

    Specifies additional include flags for the C compiler ("`-I`*directory*"). These flags can also be specified via `CFLAGS`, but for historical reasons they have their own variable.

- ### LDFLAGS
Linker Standard Flags

    Example: `LDFLAGS="-L/usr/local/lib"`

    Specifies additional standard flags for the linker command. These flags are usually "`-L`*directory*" flags intended to help the linker find third-party libraries.

- ### LIBS
Linker Library Flags

    Example: `LIBS="-ldb"`

    Specifies additional library flags for the linker command. These flags are usually just "`-l`*name*" flags for linking Apache with third-party libraries.

- ### CFLAGS_SHLIB
Additional CFLAGS for DSO Building

    Example: `CFLAGS_SHLIB="-fPIC"`

> To squeeze out the maximum on a Pentium platform, compile with "`CC=pgcc CFLAGS='-O6 -mpentium'`" when the Pentium optimized GNU C compiler is available. This option speeds up at least number-crunching tasks such as regex matching.

Special flags for the C compiler that are used in addition to CFLAGS when DSOs are compiled. Usually, they specify which flags are required to force the generation of *position-independent code* (PIC).

■ **LD_SHLIB**   Linker for DSO Building
Example: LD_SHLIB="ld"

Specifies the linker used for building DSOs. The default is platform-dependent and is usually either the value of CC or directly "ld".

In most cases, you do
not need to specify
DSO building details
manually. Apache
already knows how to
use DSO on all major
UNIX platforms.

■ **LDFLAGS_SHLIB**   Additional LDFLAGS for DSO Building
Example: LDFLAGS_SHLIB="-Bshareable"

Special flags for the DSO linker command (LD_SHLIB) that are used in addition to LDFLAGS when DSOs are built. Usually, they specify which flags are required to force the generation of shared objects instead of standard objects (executables).

■ **LDFLAGS_SHLIB_EXPORT**   Add. LDFLAGS for Program
Building under DSO
Example: LDFLAGS_SHLIB_EXPORT="-rdynamic"

Special flags for the linker command (CC) that are used in addition to LDFLAGS when the Apache executable is built. Usually, they specify which flags are required to force the export of API symbols for use by DSO-based modules.

■ **RANLIB**   Archive Indexing Tool
Example: RANLIB="/bin/true"

Used to override the "ranlib" command if the local platform doesn't require it. This command is rarely needed, because Apache automatically knows whether it is required.

■ **DEPS**   Additional Makefile Dependency
Example: DEPS="..."

For developers only. This command can be used to add a *Make* dependency to src/Makefile.

■ **TARGET**   Name of the Target Program
Example: TARGET="apache"

Equivalent to the option --target. (See this option for details.)

■ **EAPI_MM**   Path to MM Library (mod_ssl only)
Example: EAPI_MM="SYSTEM"

Sets the path to the MM library source or installation tree. This library is used in conjunction with the *Extended API* (EAPI) facility. The argument "SYSTEM" can be specified to indicate that APACI should search for the MM library in standard system locations.

■ **SSL_BASE**   Path to OpenSSL Toolkit (mod_ssl only)
Example: SSL_BASE="SYSTEM"

Sets the path to the OpenSSL toolkit source or installation tree. This toolkit is used in conjunction with mod_ssl. The string "SYSTEM" can be specified as the argument to indicate that APACI should search for the OpenSSL toolkit in standard system locations.

■ **RSA_BASE**   Path to RSAref Library (mod_ssl only)
Example: RSA_BASE="SYSTEM"

mod_ssl extends APACI; that's why additional configuration variables are available.

Sets the path to the RSAref library source or installation tree. This library is used by U.S. residents (only) in conjunction with mod_ssl. The string "SYSTEM" can be specified as the argument to indicate that APACI should search for the RSAref library in standard system locations.

3.2.2   General Options

The following general *option*s are available on the APACI command line:

■ **--quiet**   Quiet Configuration
Example: --quiet

Forces APACI to suppress the display of all output while configuring the source tree. This option can be useful for running APACI in batch mode — for instance, from a vendor packaging facility like RPM.

■ **--verbose**   Verbose Configuration
Example: --verbose

Forces APACI to display additional output while configuring the Apache source tree. This option can be useful for testing the results of various configuration options.

Use --shadow for building Apache on multiple architectures in parallel.

■ **--shadow[=*Dir*]**   Create a Shadow Source Tree
Example: --shadow=/tmp/apache

Creates a shadow tree of the Apache source tree under the specified directory *Dir* before configuration. A shadow tree consists of all directories of the original tree, with all files inside those directories being replaced by symbolic links to the original files. This option is useful when the original Apache source tree stays on a read-only medium (typically, a CD-ROM) or when one compiles Apache in parallel for multiple platforms. Details about this facility are found in section 3.3.1.

3.2.3   Stand-alone Options

The following *option*s stand alone. That is, they stop the configuration process and instead perform a special action only.

▪ **--help**   Display Usage Summary
Example: `--help`

Displays a short usage summary page listing all APACI command-line options. Use this option when you have forgotten an option and want to identify it.

▪ **--show-layout**   Display Installation Path Layout
Example: `--show-layout`

Displays the resulting installation path layout. By default, this option displays the "Apache" layout from the file `config.layout`. It is also useful in combination with the `--with-layout` option and the other installation layout options (see section 3.2.4) for easily checking the results of those options without having to configure, build, and install the package.

3.2.4   Installation Layout Options

The following *option*s are used for configuring the general installation path layout:

▪ **--with-layout=[*File*:]*Name***   Installation Path Layout
Example: `--with-layout=GNU`

The `--with-layout` option allows you to load custom installation path layouts from a file.

Selects the predefined installation path layout named *Name* from the file `config.layout`. This file includes several popular layout ingredients, and you can set all of their paths at once with this single option. The default is the historical "Apache" layout. The most typical layout is "GNU," which resembles the installation paths of typical GNU Autoconf-based packages. When the *Name* argument is prefixed with "*File*:", *Name* is loaded from *File* instead of `config.layout`. Use this option for easy loading your own custom layouts.

▪ **--target=*Name***   Installation Target Name
Example: `--target=apache`

Sets the name of the target program to *Name*. The default is the historical "httpd". This name affects both the name of the installed executable and the error messages.

■ **--prefix=***Prefix*   Installation Path Prefix
Example: `--prefix=/usr/local/apache`

As with original GNU Autoconf "configure" scripts, this option is the most important choice. It sets the installation path prefix — that is, the root of the installation tree. Because most other installation path-related options are, by default, subdirectories of this path, this option implicitly changes the value of these options unless you configure them manually. The default for *Prefix* is `/usr/local/apache`. In most cases, this option is all you need to force the installation to take place in a different file system area.

The only mandatory APACI is `--prefix`.

■ **--exec-prefix=***ExecPrefix* Installation Path Prefix for Executables
Example: `--exec-prefix=/usr/local/apache.'uname -m'`

Similar to `--prefix`, but configures only the prefixes for executables — or, more correctly, for architecture-dependent files. The default for *ExecPrefix* is *Prefix*; that is, by default APACI doesn't distinguish between the various types of files. This option is useful primarily when you install Apache for multiple architectures into the same installation area.

■ **--datadir=***DataDir*   Installation Path Prefix for Shared Data
Example: `--datadir=/usr/local/apache/share`

Sets the installation path prefix for the static, read-only data files used by Apache (such as hypertext documents, and CGI scripts). The default depends on the installation path layout (see the discussion of the `--with-layout` option), but *DataDir* usually defaults to *Prefix*; that is, this directory is usually a path prefix for other paths.

■ **--localstatedir=***StateDir*   Inst. Path Prefix for Dynamic Data
Example: `--localstatedir=/usr/local/apache/var`

Sets the installation path prefix for the various dynamic/writable data files used by Apache (such as log files). The default depends on the installation path layout (see the discussion of the `--with-layout` option), but *StateDir* usually defaults to *Prefix*; that is, this directory is usually a path prefix for other paths.

By default, APACI uses a three-step path dependency hierarchy: `--with-layout` *at the top, then a few options like* `--datadir` *that group related files, and finally specialized options like* `--bindir` *for fine-tuning.*

The following *option*s are used for fine-tuning the installation path layout:

■ **--bindir=***Dir*   Installation Path for User Binaries
Example: `--bindir=/usr/local/apache/bin`

Sets the installation path for user binaries — that is, executables that will be run by the end user. The default depends on the installation path layout (see the discussion of the `--with-layout` option), but *Dir* usually defaults to *ExecPrefix*/bin.

■ **--sbindir=***Dir*   Installation Path for System Binaries
Example: `--sbindir=/usr/local/apache/bin`

Sets the installation path for system binaries — that is, executables that will be run by system administrators only. The default depends on the installation path layout (see the discussion of the `--with-layout` option), but *Dir* usually defaults to *ExecPrefix*/`bin`.

■ **--libexecdir=***Dir*   Installation Path for Internal Binaries
Example: `--libexecdir=/usr/local/apache/libexec`

Sets the installation path for internal binaries — that is, executables and DSOs that will be loaded and run by Apache itself. The default depends on the installation path layout (see the discussion of the `--with--layout` option), but *Dir* usually defaults to *ExecPrefix*/`libexec`.

■ **--mandir=***Dir*   Installation Path for Manual Pages
Example: `--mandir=/usr/local/apache/man`

Sets the installation path for the UNIX manual pages. The default depends on the installation path layout (see the discussion of the `--with--layout` option), but *Dir* usually defaults to *Prefix*/`man`.

■ **--sysconfdir=***Dir*   Installation Path for Configuration
Example: `--sysconfdir=/usr/local/apache/etc`

Sets the installation path for the various configuration files. The default depends on the installation path layout (see the discussion of the `--with-layout` option), but *Dir* usually defaults to *Prefix*/`conf`.

Most of the APACI options are similar in name to the ones specified by the GNU standards.

■ **--includedir=***Dir*   Installation Path for C Include Files
Example: `--includedir=/usr/local/apache/include`

Sets the installation path for the C language include files (also known as "header files"), which are used by the APXS facility. The default depends on the installation path layout (see the discussion of the `--with--layout` option), but *Dir* usually defaults to *Prefix*/`include`.

■ **--iconsdir=***Dir*   Installation Path for Icons
Example: `--iconsdir=/usr/local/apache/share/icons`

Sets the installation path for icon images. The default depends on the installation path layout (see the discussion of the `--with-layout` option), but *Dir* usually defaults to *DataDir*/`icons`.

■ **--htdocsdir=***Dir*   Installation Path for Hypertext Documents
Example: `--htdocsdir=/usr/local/apache/share/htdocs`

Sets the installation path for hypertext documents. The default depends on the installation path layout (see the discussion of the `--with--layout` option), but *Dir* usually defaults to *DataDir*/`htdocs`.

■ **--cgidir=***Dir*   Installation Path for CGI Scripts
Example: `--htdocsdir=/usr/local/apache/share/cgi-bin`

Sets the installation path for CGI scripts. The default depends on the installation path layout (see the discussion of the `--with-layout` option), but *Dir* usually defaults to *DataDir*`/cgi-bin`.

■ **--runtimedir=***Dir*   Installation Path for Runtime Data
Example: `--runtimedir=/usr/local/apache/var`

Sets the installation path for the runtime data of Apache (scoreboard, PID file, and so on). The default depends on the installation path layout (see the discussion of the `--with-layout` option), but *Dir* usually defaults to *StateDir*`/logs`.

■ **--logfiledir=***Dir*   Installation Path for Log Files
Example: `--logfiledir=/usr/local/apache/var`

This sets the installation path for the log files. The default depends on the installation path layout (see the discussion of the `--with-layout` option), but *Dir* usually defaults to *StateDir*`/logs`.

■ **--proxycachedir=***Dir*   Installation Path for Proxy Cache
Example: `--proxycachedir=/usr/local/apache/var`

Sets the installation path for the proxy module's cache. The default depends on the installation path layout (see the discussion of the `--with-layout` option), but *Dir* usually defaults to *StateDir*`/proxy`.

3.2.5 Build Options

The following *option*s are used for configuring the various build parameters:

For configuring special details of Apache, some configuration rules exist. Some of them were added to APACI by `mod_ssl`.

■ **--enable-rule=***Name*   Enable a Configuration Rule
Example: `--enable-rule=WANTHSREGEX`

Used to enable various configuration rules. The following rule *Name*s are available:

SHARED_CORE   Configures the Apache core to be built into a shared library.

SHARED_CHAIN   Configures the linking of module DSOs against possibly existing shared libraries.

SOCKS4   Builds Apache with the SOCKS version 4 toolkit. When it is enabled, you must add the SOCKS library location to LIBS, otherwise, "`-L/usr/local/lib -lsocks`" will be assumed.

SOCKS5   Builds Apache with the SOCKS version 5 toolkit. When it is enabled, you must add the SOCKS library location to LIBS, otherwise, "-L/usr/local/lib -lsocks5" will be assumed.

IRIXNIS   Takes effect only if you are configuring on SGI IRIX. Read the src/Configuration.tmpl file for more details.

IRIXN32   Takes effect only if you are configuring on SGI IRIX. Read the src/Configuration.tmpl file for more details.

PARANOID   During the configuration, modules can run pre-programmed shell commands in the same environment in which APACI runs. This rule allows modules to control how APACI works. Normally, APACI will simply note that a module is performing this function. If you use this rule, it will also print out the code that the modules execute.

EXPAT   Includes James Clark's *Expat* package (an XML/1.0 parsing library) into Apache, for use by the modules. By default, this rule is already enabled.

WANTHSREGEX   Apache requires a POSIX-compliant regular expression library. Henry Spencer's excellent *Regex* package is included with Apache and is used automatically when the underlying operating system has no equivalent library. By default, this rule is enabled unless it is overruled by operating system specifics.

> If you have a broken vendor regex library (for instance, if you observe core dumps on RewriteRule directives), use --enable-rule=-WANTHSREGEX.

EAPI (mod_ssl only)   Enables EAPI, which provides a generic, low-level, function-calling mechanism, a generic data structure context mechanism; and shared memory support.

SSL_COMPAT (mod_ssl only)   Enables mod_ssl to be built with backward-compatible code for Apache-SSL 1.x, mod_ssl 2.0.x, Sioux 1.x, and Stronghold 2.x. By default, it is already enabled.

SSL_SDBM (mod_ssl only)   Controls whether the built-in SDBM library should be used for mod_ssl instead of a custom-defined or vendor-supplied DBM library. The default is to use a vendor NDBM library.

> If you have a broken vendor NDBM library (for instance, if you observe core dumps on HTTPS requests), use --enable-rule=-SSL_SDBM.

SSL_EXPERIMENTAL (mod_ssl only)   Can be used to enable experimental code inside mod_ssl. These new features typically need more testing before they can be considered stable.

SSL_VENDOR (mod_ssl only)   Can be used to enable code inside mod_ssl that product vendors can use to extend mod_ssl itself via EAPI hooks without patching the source.

■ **--disable-rule=*Name***   Disable a Configuration Rule

Example: --disable-rule=WANTHSREGEX

Disables a rule.

■ **--add-module=***Name*   Import a Third-Party Module

Example: `--add-module=/tmp/mod_foo.c`

Imports and activates a third-party module *File* into the Apache source tree under `src/modules/extra/`. See Section 3.3.2 for more details.

■ **--activate-module=***File*   Activate Third-Party Module

Example: `--activate-module=src/modules/extra/mod_foo.o`

Activates a manually imported third-party module *File*, which must stay under `src/modules/`. See Section 3.3.2 for more details.

■ **--permute-module=***Name1:Name2*   Permute Module Order

Example: `--permute-module=rewrite:alias`

An expert option that can be used to permute the order of modules. See Section 3.3.3 for more details.

■ **--enable-module=***Name*   Enable a Module for Building

Example: `--enable-module=rewrite`

Enables a module "mod_*Name*" for building. The following modules are available (a "★" indicates that it is enabled by default):

> Use the powerful
> `--enable-module` and
> `--disable-module`
> options to assemble
> your individual Apache
> functionality.

`http_core ★`	`mod_dir ★`	`mod_asis ★`
`mod_so`	`mod_actions ★`	`mod_autoindex ★`
`mod_alias ★`	`mod_negotiation ★`	`mod_status ★`
`mod_rewrite`	`mod_env ★`	`mod_info`
`mod_userdir ★`	`mod_setenvif ★`	`mod_log_config ★`
`mod_imap ★`	`mod_unique_id`	`mod_log_agent`
`mod_speling`	`mod_cgi ★`	`mod_log_referer`
`mod_access ★`	`mod_include ★`	`mod_usertrack`
`mod_auth ★`	`mod_mime ★`	`mod_mmap_static`
`mod_auth_anon`	`mod_mime_magic`	`mod_example`
`mod_auth_dbm`	`mod_expires`	`mod_proxy`
`mod_auth_db`	`mod_headers`	`mod_perl`
`mod_digest`	`mod_cern_meta`	`mod_ssl`

Two special variants of *Name* exist: "`all`" enables all existing modules and "`most`" enables only those modules known to be usable on all platforms without problems.

■ **--disable-module=***Name*   Disable a Module for Building

Example: `--disable-module=alias`

Disables an enabled (by default or manually) module from building.

■ **--enable-shared=***Name*   Enable a Module for DSO

Example: `--enable-shared=rewrite`

Enables a module "mod_*Name*" for building as a DSO. In addition to the standard module names, two special variants of *Name* exist: "max" enables DSO for all modules except for the bootstrapping modules (http_core and mod_so), and "remain" first enables all still-disabled modules, then enables them for building as a DSO.

■ **--disable-shared=***Name*   Disable a Module for DSO
Example: --disable-shared=rewrite

Disables a module "mod_*Name*" for building as a DSO.

■ **--with-perl=***File*   Sets the Perl Interpreter
Example: --with-perl=/usr/local/bin/perl

Sets the path to the Perl interpreter executable to *File*. By default, APACI searches for "perl" and "perl5" in $PATH for the latest interpreter version. Use this option when more than one Perl interpreter is installed on your system or you want to use a Perl interpreter found in a nonstandard file system location.

■ **--without-support**   Build without Support Tools
Example: --without-support

Forces APACI to not build the support tools under src/support/. By default, these tools are built. Use this option when these tools are unnecessary cause portability problems.

■ **--without-confadjust**   No Configuration Adjustments
Example: --without-confadjust

Vendor package maintainers should keep --without--confadjust in mind.

Forces APACI to not adjust the configuration files on installation. By default, APACI recognizes, for instance, that when you build as non-root (UID ≠ 0), it might be reasonable to pre-configure Apache for port 8080 instead of 80 (because non-root users cannot run Apache on port 80). Sometimes these adjustments are confusing, especially for vendor package maintainers. In such a case, you can disable the adjustments with this option.

■ **--without-execstrip**   No Executable Stripping
Example: --without-execstrip

Forces APACI to not "strip" (remove debugging symbols) the executables when installing them. This option can be either useful for debugging purposes or required on esoteric platforms where the DSO facility works only when the Apache executable is not "stripped."

3.2.6   suEXEC Options

The following *option*s for configuring the suEXEC facility are available on the APACI command line:

- **--enable-suexec**   Enables suEXEC Facility
  Example: `--enable-suexec`

  Enables the suEXEC facility, which can be used to run CGI scripts under particular UIDs.

- **--suexec-caller=***Name*   suEXEC Caller UID
  Example: `--suexec-caller=www`

  Sets the user name of the suEXEC calling process to *Name* — that is, the UID under which Apache *runs* (when Apache is started as root, so that UID = 0, the *Name* can be a configured custom UID; see the User directive). The suEXEC then runs only CGI scripts when the calling process has this user name.

- **--suexec-docroot=***Dir*   suEXEC Document Root
  Example: `--suexec-docroot=/usr/local/apache/share/htdocs`

  Sets the path for the suEXEC document root to *Dir*.

- **--suexec-logfile=***File*   suEXEC Log File Path
  Example: `--suexec-logfile=/usr/local/apache/var/suexec.log`

  Sets the path for the dedicated suEXEC log file to *File*.

- **--suexec-userdir=***SubDir*   suEXEC User Home Subdirectory
  Example: `--suexec-userdir=.public-html`

  Sets *SubDir* as the subdirectory of the user's "homedirs," where CGI scripts must reside to be executed through suEXEC.

- **--suexec-uidmin=***UID*   suEXEC Minimum UID
  Example: `--suexec-uidmin=1024`

  Sets the minimum UNIX user ID to *UID*; the suEXEC facility can then switch to it.

- **--suexec-gidmin=***GID*   suEXEC Minimum GID
  Example: `--suexec-gidmin=1024`

  Sets the minimum UNIX group ID to *GID*; the suEXEC facility can then switch to it.

- **--suexec-safepath=***Path*   suEXEC Safe PATH Variable
  Example: `--suexec-safepath=/bin:/usr/bin`

  Enforces the colon-separated `$PATH` variable to *Path* for use under the suEXEC facility.

> The suEXEC facility allows CGI scripts to be executed under the UID/GID of the script owner instead of the runtime UID/GID of the Apache server processes.

3.3   Configuration Special Topics

The final section of this chapter examines some special configuration issues on which we've touched only tangentially in previous discussions.

3.3.1   Shadow Source Trees

The `--shadow[=`*Dir*`]` option is very interesting. It can be used to build Apache inside a temporary location without copying the entire Apache source tree (15MB in size). This option is useful mainly in two situations. First, you can use it when you want to build Apache on a cluster of machines in parallel and want to avoid conflicts (the source then generally stays on an NFS-mounted file system). Second, when the Apache source tree resides on a read-only file system (typically a CD-ROM), you must ensure that the build process can write the object files. Both problems are efficiently resolved through shadow trees.

A shadow tree consists of a copy of all directories of the original tree, but with all files inside these directories being replaced by symbolic links to the original files. Such a tree can be created more quickly than a direct tree copy can, and it requires less disk space. You simply specify an additional `--shadow` option on the APACI command line, and Apache automatically builds inside this tree in the background.

Shadow trees may be employed in two ways:

■ You can specify only "`--shadow`". In this case, the shadow tree is made only for the `src/` subdirectory of the Apache source tree and placed side-by-side to this directory. It is named "`src.`*platform*", where *platform* is the platform identification string. Use this option when you want to build for multiple architectures in parallel.

The flexibility of Apache means that one can easily add third-party modules to extend Apache's functionality.

■ You can specify "`--shadow=`*Dir*". In this case, the shadow tree is made for the entire Apache source tree and placed under *Dir*. Use this option when you want to build from a read-only media.

3.3.2   On-the-Fly Addition of Third-Party Modules

As you may have recognized in our example installation (Section 3.1 on page 37), third-party modules can be added to the Apache source tree in three ways:

■ They can be automatically added and activated by a script. For instance, `mod_ssl` uses this approach.

■ They can be automatically added by a script but activated manually by the user. For instance, mod_perl uses this approach.

■ They can be manually added and activated by the user. Most Apache modules provided by third parties use this approach.

This little inconsistency arises because larger modules have more requirements; to make the life of the user easier, these modules partly automate the steps. Don't be alarmed if the complex modules differ. The basic way for manually adding a third-party module in APACI involves three steps:

1. Obtain the module source. For small modules, it is typically a mod_foo-.c source file. For larger modules, it may be a directory containing at least Makefile.tmpl, mod_bar.c, and a few additional source files (conventionally named bar_xxx.c).

   Third-party modules differ mainly in size: either they are single source modules or they are contained in their own directory.

2. Add the module source to the Apache source tree somewhere under src/modules. The location selected depends on the module. With a single mod_foo.c, you usually place the source under src/modules/-extra/ by using --add-module=/path/to/foo/mod_foo.c. For larger modules that require their own subdirectory under src/modules/ (say, src/modules/bar), you must establish this directory manually by running "cp -rp /path/to/bar/ src/modules/bar/" and later activate it by using --activate-module=src/modules/bar/libbar.a.

3. Once the third-party modules are fully integrated into the source tree of Apache, you can treat them just like the distributed modules. In both cases, you enable the module for building via --enable-module=foo or --enable-module=bar. The same idea applies when building as a DSO: a simple --enable-shared=foo or --enable-shared=bar is all that is needed.

3.3.3 Module Order and Permutations

You may have recognized the harmless-looking APACI option --permute--module=*Name1*:*Name2*. We briefly mentioned that it can be used for changing the order of modules. To fully understand this option and its utility, more knowledge of Apache internals are required.

As explained in Chapter 2, the functionality of Apache is implemented by modules. An API dispatches the HTTP request processing. During this dispatching a fixed module order is used that is derived from the order employed when building the modules. Actually, it mirrors the order of the AddModule/SharedModule lines in the file src/Configuration.apaci, which APACI generates from src/Configuration.tmpl. When a module

Use –permutemodule to change the module order at installation time and the execution order at runtime.

comes later in this file, it is dispatched earlier in the processing. For instance, mod_rewrite comes after mod_alias in this file, so mod_rewrite gets control for each API step before mod_alias. As a result, mod_rewrite can manipulate URLs before mod_alias can, but it cannot override results of mod_alias.

For all distributed modules, the order is pre-configured in a reasonable way. Nevertheless, sometimes you may want to change the order of one or more modules. For instance, to give mod_alias higher priority over mod_rewrite, you would use the following:

```
$   ./configure ... --permute-module=alias:rewrite ...
```

Now mod_rewrite can post-process URLs that were manipulated by mod_alias. On the other hand, when you add a third-party module, it is always appended to the end of src/Configuration.apaci; hence, it gets the highest priority by default. This order often isn't reasonable. For instance, when you have added another URL manipulation module (say, mod_foo), it might be reasonable to ensure that it operates after mod_rewrite and mod_alias. This goal can be achieved by using the following APACI command line:

```
$   ./configure ... --add-module=/path/to/mod_foo.c --permute-module=foo:BEGIN ...
```

This command moves mod_foo to the beginning of the module list and gives it the lowest priority. More complex module order adjustments can be achieved by combining multiple --permute-module options.

Chapter 4

Configuring Apache

Build a system that even a fool can use,
and only a fool will want to use it.
— Shaw's Principle

I n this chapter we present a concise but quite complete reference for all of the configuration directives that Apache provides to both the webmaster (in the global server configuration files) and users (in the per-directory configuration files). First, we give a brief description of the various resource identifiers used by the directives. Next, then we introduce the configuration scopes in which directives can occur. Finally, we describe all available directives, grouped by the same topics as used in Chapter 2.

4.1 Configuration Terminology

4.1.1 Resource Identifiers

The various Apache configuration directives use a number of resource identifiers to reference external things. Because they are all related and can be discovered as parts of the *Uniform Resource Locator* (URL), we summarize them in a single figure (Figure 4.1 on the next page).

Apache configuration directives use URLs and their subidentifiers to reference resources.

Host name, domain name, FQDN: The *host name* is a case-insensitive alphanumerical string that identifies a particular machine. The *domain name*

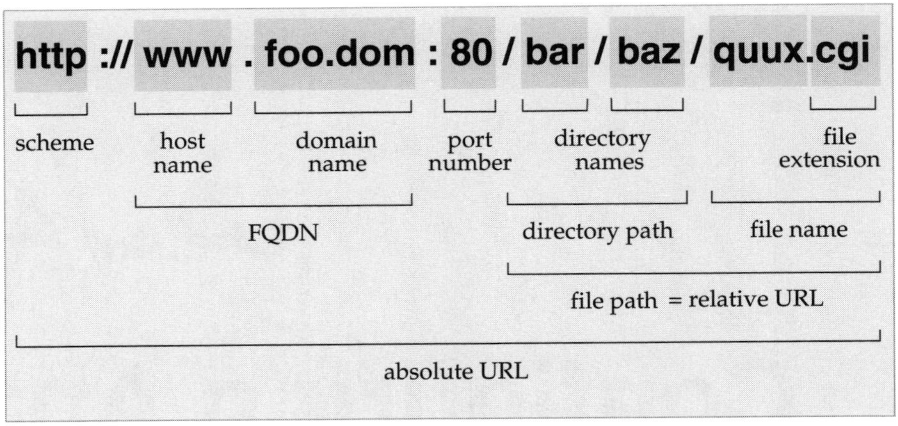

Figure 4.1: The resource identifiers used by Apache directives

is the concatenation (with dot-characters) of case-insensitive alphanumerical strings that identify the path from the top-level domain to the sublevel domain in the Domain Name System (DNS) to which the machine belongs. The Fully Qualified Domain Name (FQDN) is just the dot-concatenation of a *host name* and its corresponding *domain name*.

A host name identifies a particular machine on the network.

Directory name, directory path: A *directory path* identifies the location in a hierarchical storage system and is simply the concatenation (by using slash characters) of one or more case-sensitive alphanumerical *directory names*. In a special case, the first directory (the "root directory") is treated as an empty name.

A directory path identifies the location in a hierarchical storage system.

File name, file extension, file path, relative URL: A *file name* is a case-sensitive alphanumerical string of a file in a storage system that can optionally consist of a base name and a *file extension*. The *file path* or *relative URL* is the *file name* prefixed with its corresponding *directory path*.

Scheme, port number, absolute URL: An *absolute URL* uniquely identifies a resource in the hierarchical space of the World Wide Web (WWW) by prefixing the host-specific *relative URL* with the FQDN (p.60) and *port number* on which the resource providing service identified by a *scheme* resides.

A URL identifies the location in the hierarchical space of the World Wide Web.

4.1.2   Pattern Matching Notations

Apache uses two classical notations for pattern matching on strings: *Wildcard Pattern* matching and *Regular Expression* matching as specified in POSIX 1003.2. The two differ in terms of concept and complexity, but use a very similar syntax. It is therefore especially important that one remembers the difference between them.

Characters (items matching fixed text)	
c	Matches the particular character c (*plain text*)
$\backslash c$	Matches the particular character c (*escaped text*)
Meta Characters (items matching variable text)	
?	Matches an arbitrary single character (*small wildcard*)
*	Matches none or any number of arbitrary characters (*large wildcard*)
$[c_1 c_2 \cdots c_n]$	Matches one character of $c_1, c_2, \ldots, c_n$ (*character class*)
$[^\wedge c_1 c_2 \cdots c_n]$	Matches one character not of $c_1, c_2, \ldots, c_n$ (*negated character class*)

Table 4.1: Wildcard Patterns Syntax

Wildcard Patterns   *Wildcard Patterns* are easy to understand and are summarized in Table 4.1. They provide meta-characters, which allow one to collapse parts of URLs and file paths.

Inside Apache, a special rule typically applies to the wildcard characters "?" and "*": they do not match a slash character ("/") when they are used to match URLs and file paths, which closely mimics the behavior of UNIX shells.

Additionally, a shorthand notation for character classes exists, reflecting the fact that in most code maps at least the alphanumerical characters are located in sequence. You can therefore use a range construct; for instance, instead of "`[abcdefghijklmnopqrstuvwxyz0123456789]`", you can write the shorter and more intuitive variant "`[a-z0-9]`".

> Wildcard Patterns provide meta-characters, which allow one to collapse parts of URLs and file paths.

Regular Expressions   While *Wildcard Patterns* are a simple concept that is well known from the various UNIX shells, they are often a too weak concept to satisfy more complex matching requirements. *Regular Expressions* fill this gap. They use a very similar syntax, but totally different semantics.[1] Table 4.2 on the next page shows the classical syntax supported inside Apache. Regular Expressions are more powerful than Wildcard Patterns because they

> Wildcard Patterns are a too weak concept to satisfy more complex matching requirements. Regular Expressions fill this gap.

---

[1] In Wildcard Patterns, the characters "?" and "*" are *jokers* that stand on their own; in Regular Expressions, these characters are just *qualifiers* that cannot stand on their own. Instead, they apply to the previous characters. The general equivalent of "`foo*`" in Regular Expression syntax, for example, is "`foo.*`" and not "`foo*`" (which would match "`fo`" followed by zero or more "`o`" characters!). Additionally, when you take the rule into account that "*" doesn't match a slash in various situations, then the equivalent Regular Expression in this context actually is "`[^/]*`". The same applies to "?", of course.

Characters (items matching fixed text)	
c	Matches the particular character c (*plain text*)
$\backslash c$	Matches the particular character c (*escaped text*)
Meta Characters (items matching variable text)	
.	Matches an arbitrary single character (*joker*)
$[c_1 c_2 \cdots c_n]$	Matches one character of $c_1, c_2, \ldots, c_n$ (*character class*)
$[\hat{}\,c_1 c_2 \cdots c_n]$	Matches one character not of $c_1, c_2, \ldots, c_n$ (*negated character class*)
Quantifiers (items appended to provide counting)	
?	One allowed, but is optional $(0, 1)$
*	Any number allowed, but are optional $(0, 1, \ldots)$
+	One required, additional are optional $(1, 2, \ldots)$
$\{min, max\}$	*Min* required, *Max* allowed (*min*, . . . ,*max*)
Anchors (items matching positions)	
$\hat{}$	Begin of string
$	End of string
Specials (items with special semantics)	
. . . | . . .	Matches either expression it separates (*alternation*)
(. . .)	Limits scope of alternation, provides grouping for quantifiers and "captures" for back-references

Table 4.2: Regular Expressions Syntax

are actually a notation for a complete regular grammar that provides a powerful facility to describe a character sequence. The drawback is that humans often find the notation difficult to decipher. Nevertheless, Regular Expressions are very important, because they can be evaluated very efficiently.

4.2   Configuration Structure

4.2.1   Configuration Files

The drawback of Regular Expressions is that humans often find their notation difficult to decipher.

Apache uses a dedicated global configuration file that, by default, is named `httpd.conf` and stays in the `conf/` directory under the *server root* (the file name can be overridden by the `-f` option on the `httpd` command line). This file is processed once on the server's start-up and then again on every server restart.[2]

---

[2]For historical reasons related to multiple initialization rounds, Apache actually reads the configuration file twice on start-up, though the process remains invisible to the user. It's one reason that makes some modules like `mod_perl` and `mod_ssl` so complex and forces them and their developers to fight against the

Historically, two other files were read in addition to `httpd.conf`: `access-.conf` (containing only access control directives) and `srm.conf` (for the *server resource map*, which contains all forms of resource configuration directives). Their file names can be overridden with the `AccessConfig` and `Resource-Config` directives in `httpd.conf`. The use of these two files has been deprecated since Apache 1.3, however, so one should generally use "`AccessConfig /dev/null`" and "`ResourceConfig /dev/null`" and place all per-server directives in the `httpd.conf` file.

Apache can also be configured on a per-directory basis by local configuration files, by default named `.htaccess`. These files are taken into account when the `AllowOverride` directives in the per-server context support them. They are then processed when Apache walks through the file system hierarchy to find the requested documents. The processing takes the path shown in Figure 4.2.

> The `.htaccess` files are processed while Apache walks through the file system hierarchy to find the requested documents.

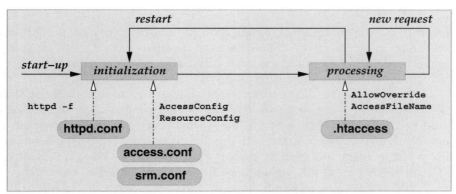

Figure 4.2: Processing of configuration files

Background Information:

Apache is derived from the *NCSA HTTP Server*, which uses these three configuration files and strongly distinguishes between them. The `httpd.conf` was its general server configuration, the `access.conf` contained only real access control directives, and the `srm.conf` contained only resource configuration directives.

Apache never made a strong distinction between these three files, however. Since the earliest versions of Apache, all three files were treated equally and could contain the same type of directives. The support for two extra configuration files was kept just for backward-compatibility reasons. This support often caused confusion, so the Apache Group finally decided to officially declare the use of the two extra configuration files as deprecated.

> Since the earliest versions of Apache, all three configuration files were treated equally and could contain the same type of directives.

Of course, the splitting of `httpd.conf` into separate files is not deprecated in general. It's often needed and a good idea to use this approach. For this purpose, Apache provides the more general `Include` directive, which is an explicit approach. What's deprecated is the implicit approach of the two special configuration file names and the fact that they're used implicitly.

---

subtle side effects of this approach.

4.2.2   Configuration Grammar

The general structure of Apache configuration files is easy to understand, because Apache defines only the framework and some sectioning rules. The available (and sometimes far from easy to understand) directives and their allowed arguments are fully implemented and controlled by the Apache modules. Thus, in general, an Apache configuration file's structure can be described with the following first fragment of a syntax grammar:

Apache defines only the framework for configuration files.

configuration	::=	*directive**
directive	::=	*section-directive* | *simple-directive*
section-directive	::=	*section-open* **configuration** *section-close*
section-open	::=	*"<" directive-name directive-argument* ">"*
section-close	::=	*"< /" directive-name ">"*
simple-directive	::=	*directive-name directive-argument**
directive-name	::=	*"Directory" | "DocumentRoot" | ···*
directive-argument	::=	*···*

An Apache configuration file can be empty or can consist of one or more directives.

In other words, an Apache configuration file can be empty or can consist of one or more directives. Directives are classified into one of two categories: simple directives and sectioning directives. Sectioning directives can, in turn, contain one or more directives.

Apache parses and evaluates the configuration files on a line-by-line basis, but allows line continuation.

Although the preceding grammar may suggest structural complexity, the actual syntax of those configuration files is very simple, because they are read and parsed by Apache on a line-by-line basis[3]: Every line that isn't empty (that is, does not match the regular expression "^[\t]*$") and is not a commentary line (that is, does not match "^[\t]*#.*$") is treated as a directive line. On those lines, the first word is treated as the *directive-name* and any remaining words form the *directive-arguments*. Additionally, when the line ends with a back slash ("\"), the following line is treated as a continuation of the current line (when this continuation line again contains a back slash, it's also part of the continuation, and so forth).

4.2.3   Configuration Contexts

Not all Apache configuration directives can be used everywhere. Apache distinguishes between the following configuration contexts on a per-directive basis (that is, every directive has a fixed set of contexts in which it is allowed as shown in Figure 4.3 on the next page).

---

[3] Actually Apache *evaluates* the directives on this line-by-line basis, although the general structure is a nested one (notice the recursion through *configuration* in the grammar!). That's surprising at the time of first reading and scary at the second time, especially when you have knowledge of compiler construction.

You can imagine that some tricks and limitations affect Apache's ability to evaluate the logically nested structure on such a physically line-by-line basis. Even when you see nicely nested <VirtualHost> and <Directory> sections in configuration files and would expect deeply nested internal syntax trees, realize that Apache internally treats the whole matter as more or less flat text.

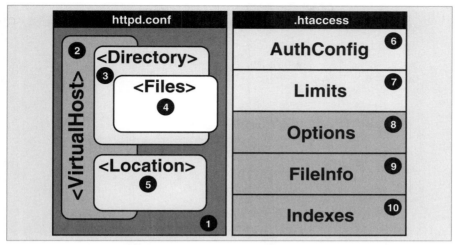

Figure 4.3: Configuration contexts

■ **Per-Server Context**
This context applies to the global `httpd.conf` configuration file. It is divided into five sub-contexts:

❶ **Global context** (outside any sections):
Contains directives that are applied to the default or main server and (depending on the particular directive) may be inherited by other sections.

❷ **Virtual host sections** (<VirtualHost>):
Contain directives that are applied to a particular virtual server, and are distinguished by unique (*IP address*, *IP port*) pairs.

❸ **Directory sections** (<Directory>, <DirectoryMatch>):
Contain directives that are applied to a particular directory (and its subdirectories), and are distinguished either by plain directory paths or regular expressions matching directory paths.

❹ **File sections** (<Files>, <FilesMatch>):
Contain directives that are applied to particular files, and are distinguished by either plain file names or regular expressions matching file names.

❺ **URL sections** (<Location>, <LocationMatch>)
Contain directives that are applied to a particular URL and its sub-areas, and are distinguished by either plain relative URLs or regular expressions matching relative URLs.

■ **Per-Directory Context**

This context applies to the local .htaccess configuration files. They are read on the fly by Apache while it's walking inside the file system to process the HTTP request. This context is also divided into five sub-contexts, which are enabled with the AllowOverride directive in the httpd.conf file:

> ❻ **Authentication context** (AuthConfig):
> Contains directives that control authorization.
>
> ❼ **Limit context** (Limits):
> Contains directives that control access restrictions.
>
> ❽ **Option context** (Options):
> Contains directives that control specific directory features.
>
> ❾ **File information context** (FileInfo):
> Contains directives that control document attributes.
>
> ❿ **Index context** (Indexes):
> Contains directives that control directory indexing.

The .htaccess configuration files are read on the fly by Apache while it's walking inside the file system to process the HTTP request.

Figure 4.3 summarizes this context topology. Small versions of this figure are used later in this chapter to intuitively describe the allowed contexts of each directive.

4.2.4   Context Nesting

As shown symbolically on the left side of Figure 4.3 on the preceding page, the various configuration sections can be nested. This nesting is not arbitrary, however. Instead, the following rules apply and should be remembered:

The Apache configuration sections can be nested, albeit with a few restrictions.

> ■ The <Directory> sections are not allowed inside <Limit>, <Loca-tion>, <Files>, or any other <Directory> sections.
>
> ■ The <Location> sections are not allowed inside <Limit>, <Direc-tory>, <Files>, or any other <Location> sections.
>
> ■ The <Files> sections are not allowed inside <Limit> and <Loca-tion> sections.
>
> ■ The <Directory> and <Location> sections are not allowed inside .htaccess files, but <Files> sections are.

The canonical (and allowed nesting) to which you should force yourself is shown below (intermediate levels in this tree may be skipped, of course):

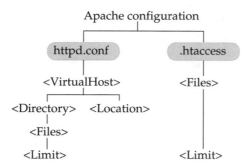

4.2.5   Context Dependencies and Implications

Although directives can be used in various contexts, some contexts implicitly include others. Two rules apply here:

- The .htaccess file contexts *AuthConfig* and *Limit* always include the contexts of the per-server <Directory>, <Files>, and <Location> sections.

- The .htaccess file contexts *Options*, *FileInfo*, and *Indexes* always include all contexts of the per-server configuration (the whole httpd-.conf file).

Additionally, the allowed directives for the <Location> and <Files> contexts are treated the same as those for <Directory>.

4.2.6   Context Merging and Inheritance

The configuration contexts have special runtime dependencies, because the results and behavior of the configuration directives (which are internally built up by the modules when a directive line is processed) become merged when Apache processes the various contexts. To understand where and why a directive is applied, it's therefore important to know the order in which Apache processes the configuration contexts (especially because the order Apache chooses is far away from intuitive or obvious):

The behaviors of the configuration directives become merged when Apache processes the configuration contexts.

1. Contexts of the <Directory> (not based on regular expressions) sections and .htaccess files are processed simultaneously, with the .htaccess directives overriding the directives of the <Directory> sections.

2. <DirectoryMatch> sections and regular expression-based <Directory> sections are processed.

3. Processing of <Files> and <FilesMatch> sections occurs simultaneously.

4. <Location> and <LocationMatch> sections are processed simultaneously.

The configuration
sections are mainly
processed in the order
in which they appear in
the configuration files.

Apart from <Directory> sections, each section group is processed in the order in which it appears in the configuration files. <Directory> is processed moving from the shortest directory component to the longest. If multiple <Directory> sections apply to the same directory, then they are processed in the configuration file order.

This nonintuitive processing has various side effects. One should always remember the following four points:

- When attempting to match objects at the file system level, you must use <Directory> and/or <Files>. To match objects at the URL level, you must use <Location>.

Although URLs come
before file system
paths from the user's
point of view,
<Location> is
processed last.

- Although URLs come before file system paths from the user's point of view, <Location> is processed last. Sections inside <VirtualHost> sections are applied after the corresponding sections outside the virtual host definition. This approach allows virtual hosts to override the main server configuration. On the other hand, modifying .htaccess parsing with the AllowOverride Options directives during <Location> accomplishes nothing because .htaccess parsing has already occurred.

- Using an Options directive inside a <Files> section has no effect.

- During runtime, Apache actually performs <Location> and <LocationMatch> sequences just before the name translation phase of the API takes place (where Alias, RewriteRule, DocumentRoot, and similar directives are used to map URLs to file names). The results of this sequence are thrown away after the translation phase ends, however.

4.3   Configuration Reference

This section presents all of the currently accepted configuration directives (255 in total), sorted by the same topics used for the module summary in Chapter 2. For each directive, a one-line summary, syntax, example, implementing module, allowed configuration contexts, and short description are given. The contents are partly derived from the Apache online documentation, courtesy of the Apache Software Foundation (ASF).

4.3.1 Core Functionality

http_core
Apache Base Functionality

■ **<VirtualHost>**   **http_core**
Open a Virtual Host Section
Syntax: <VirtualHost *target* [*target* ...]>
Example: <VirtualHost www.foo.dom:80>
Default: None
Since: Apache 1.0

This directive opens a section enclosing a group of directives that will apply one or more virtual hosts matching the *target*. Any directive that is allowed in a virtual host context may be used. When the server receives a request for a document on a particular virtual host, it uses the configuration directives enclosed in the <VirtualHost> section. The *target* argument can be either the IP address of a virtual host or an FQDN for the IP address of a virtual host.

Virtual Host sections are used to provide multiple virtual web servers on the same machine; all virtual hosts can share a part of their configuration.

The name "_default_" can be specified for *target*, in which case the section matches any IP address that is not explicitly listed in another virtual host section. In the absence of any "_default_" virtual host sections, the "main" server config, consisting of all definitions outside any <VirtualHost> section, is used when no match exists.

One can add "*:port*" to the *target* arguments to change the port for which a match is sought. If the port is unspecified, then the default is the same port indicated in the most recent Port statement of the main server. You may also specify "*:**" to match all ports on an address that is recommended when used with "_default_".

In most cases, *target* arguments correspond to the arguments of Listen directives, but not always.

■ **</VirtualHost>**   **http_core**
Close a Virtual Host Section
Syntax: </VirtualHost>
Example: </VirtualHost>
Default: None
Since: Apache 1.0

This directive closes a section previously opened by <VirtualHost>.

■ **<Location>**   **http_core**
Open a URL Location Section
Syntax: <Location *url*>
Example: <Location /status>
Default: None
Since: Apache 1.1

The <Location>
containers limit the
scope of their body to
particular URL paths.

This directive opens a section enclosing a group of directives that will apply to the named *url* and subareas of it. Any directive that is allowed in a directory context may be used. The *url* argument is either a *relative URL* or a *wildcard pattern* for a *relative URL*. If multiple <Location> sections match a location (or its parent locations) containing a document, then the sections are applied in the order beginning with the shortest match first.

■ **</Location>**   **http_core**
Close a URL Location Section
Syntax: </Location>
Example: </Location>
Default: None
Since: Apache 1.1

The directive closes a section previously opened by <Location>.

■ **<LocationMatch>**   **http_core**
Open a URL Location Section (RegEx-based)
Syntax: <LocationMatch *pattern*>
Example: <LocationMatch>
Default: None
Since: Apache 1.3

Use
<LocationMatch>
instead of
<Location> if you
want to specify the
scope more flexibly.

This directive opens a section enclosing a group of directives that will apply to those URLs matched by *pattern* and subareas of them. It is similar to <Location> with one exception: the argument (*pattern*) is a full-featured regular expression and not just a *wildcard pattern*.

■ **</LocationMatch>**   **http_core**
Close a URL Location Section (RegEx-based)
Syntax: </LocationMatch>
Example: </LocationMatch>
Default: None
Since: Apache 1.3

This directive closes a section previously opened by a corresponding <LocationMatch>.

- ▓ **\<Directory\>** **http_core**
  Open a Directory Section
  Syntax: \<Directory *directory*\>
  Example: \<Directory /usr/local/apache/htdocs\>
  Default: None
  Since: Apache 1.0

  This directive opens a section enclosing a group of directives that will apply to the named *directory* and subdirectories of it. Any directive that is allowed in a directory context may be used. The *directory* argument is either a *directory path* or a *wildcard pattern* for a *directory path*. If multiple \<Directory\> sections match a directory (or its parent directories) containing a document, then the sections are applied in order beginning with the shortest match first, interspersed with the directives from the .htaccess files along the path to the directory.

The \<Directory\> containers limit the scope of their body to particular file system paths.

- ▓ **\</Directory\>** **http_core**
  Close a Directory Section
  Syntax: \</Directory\>
  Example: \</Directory\>
  Default: None
  Since: Apache 1.0

  This directive closes a section previously opened by a corresponding \<Directory\>.

- ▓ **\<DirectoryMatch\>** **http_core**
  Open a Directory Section (RegEx-based)
  Syntax: \<DirectoryMatch *pattern*\>
  Example: \<DirectoryMatch ↑/u/[a-zA-Z0-9_]+/\>
  Default: None
  Since: Apache 1.3

  This directive opens a section enclosing a group of directives that will apply to those directories matched by *pattern* and subdirectories of them. It is similar to \<Directory\> with two exceptions: the argument (*pattern*) is a full-featured regular expression and not just a *wildcard pattern*, and the section is applied after *all* regular \<Directory\> sections are applied.

Use \<DirectoryMatch\> instead of \<Directory\> if you want to specify the scope more flexibly.

- ▓ **\</DirectoryMatch\>** **http_core**
  Close a Directory Section (RegEx-based)
  Syntax: \</DirectoryMatch\>
  Example: \</DirectoryMatch\>
  Default: None
  Since: Apache 1.3

This directive closes a section previously opened by a corresponding
<DirectoryMatch>.

■ **<Files>**   **http_core**
Open a Files Section
Syntax: <Files *file*>
Example: <Files *.html>
Default: None
Since: Apache 1.2

The <Files>
containers limit the
scope of their body to
particular file names.

This directive opens a section enclosing a group of directives that will
apply to the named *file*. Any directive that is allowed in a file's scope
may be used. The *file* argument is either a *base name* or a *wildcard pattern* for a *base name*. If multiple <Files> sections match a file, then the
sections are applied in the order in which they appear in the configuration file. A <Files> section is applied after all <Directory> sections
are applied.

■ **</Files>**   **http_core**
Close a Files Section
Syntax: </Files>
Example: </Files>
Default: None
Since: Apache 1.2

This directive closes a section previously opened by a corresponding
<Files>.

■ **<FilesMatch>**   **http_core**
Open a Files Section (RegEx-based)
Syntax: <FilesMatch *pattern*>
Example: <FilesMatch .*\.([sp]?html|cgi)$>
Default: None
Since: Apache 1.3

Use <FilesMatch>
instead of <Files> if
you want to specify the
scope more flexibly.

This directive opens a section enclosing a group of directives that will
apply to those files matched by *pattern*. It is similar to <Files> with
two exceptions: the argument (*pattern*) is a full-featured regular expression and not just a *wildcard pattern*, and the section is applied after
all regular <Files> sections are applied.

■ **</FilesMatch>**   **http_core**
Close a Files Section
Syntax: </FilesMatch>
Example: </FilesMatch>
Default: None
Since: Apache 1.3

This directive closes a section previously opened by a corresponding <FilesMatch>.

■ <Limit>   **http_core**

Open a Limitation Section
Syntax: <Limit *method* [*method* ...]>
Example: <Limit GET POST>
Default: None
Since: Apache 1.0

This directive opens a section enclosing a group of directives that will apply to the specified HTTP access methods given in *method*. The *method* argument is case-sensitive and usually GET, POST, PUT, DELETE, CONNECT, OPTIONS, or another access method. If multiple <Limit> sections match a location (or its parent locations) containing a document, then the sections are applied in order beginning with the shortest match first. To limit all methods, omit all <Limit> sections.

Use <Limit> to limit the directive scope to particular HTTP access methods.

■ </Limit>   **http_core**

Close a Limitation Section
Syntax: </Limit>
Example: </Limit>
Default: None
Since: Apache 1.0

This directive closes a section previously opened by a

■ <IfDefine>   **http_core**

Open a Define Section
Syntax: <IfDefine *name*>
Example: <IfDefine SSL>
Default: None
Since: Apache 1.3

This directive opens a section enclosing a group of directives that will apply when the command-line define *name* exists, that is, when Apache was started with the command-line option "-D*name*". The *name* argument can be preceded by an exclamation point ("!") to indicate a negated section (which applies only when the define does not exist). This feature is intended to provide a way to start-up multiple Apache server instances with the same configuration file and to provide a way to conditionally load DSO-based modules.

<IfDefine> in conjunction with LoadModule allows you to conditionally load and use modules on demand.

◼ </IfDefine>   **http_core**
Close a Define Section
Syntax: </IfDefine>
Example: </IfDefine>
Default: None
Since: Apache 1.3

This directive closes a section previously opened by a corresponding
<IfDefine>.

◼ <IfModule>   **http_core**
Open a Module Existence Section
Syntax: <IfModule *src-name*>
Example: <IfModule>
Default: None
Since: Apache 1.2

Use <IfModule> if
you want to enable
directives only if their
implementing module
is actually available.

This directive opens a section enclosing a group of directives that will
apply when the module with source name *src-name* exists — that is,
when Apache was either statically built with this module or the module was at least loaded via LoadModule. Keep in mind that *src-name*
is the file name of the main module's C source file. For instance, for
mod_foo the argument *src-name* is usually mod_foo.c. The argument
src-name can be preceded by an exclamation point ("!") to indicate a
negated section (which applies only when the module does not exist).
This feature is intended to provide a way to use certain directives only
when the module that implements them is actually available.

◼ </IfModule>   **http_core**
Close a Module Existence Section
Syntax: </IfModule>
Example: </IfModule>
Default: None
Since: Apache 1.2

This directive closes a section previously opened by a corresponding
<IfModule>.

◼ **AccessConfig**   **http_core**
Extra Access Configuration File (Deprecated)
Syntax: AccessConfig *file*
Example: AccessConfig /dev/null
Default: AccessConfig conf/access.conf
Since: Apache 1.0

Apache will read *file* for more directives after reading the ResourceConfig file. Here, the argument *file* is relative to the ServerRoot. Historically, this file contained only <Directory> sections in NCSA httpd (the ancestor of Apache); since the early Apache days, however, it was able to use *any* server directive allowed in the server configuration context. Thus this directive has been officially deprecated since Apache 1.3 and is usually disabled using "AccessConfig /dev/null".

- **AccessFileName**   **http_core**
Name of Per-Directory Configuration Files
Syntax: AccessFileName *filename*
Example: AccessFileName .apacherc
Default: AccessFileName .htaccess
Since: Apache 1.0

When returning a document to the client, Apache looks for the first existing access control file from this list of names in every directory of the path to the document, if access control files are enabled for that directory. For instance, before returning the document /usr/local/web/-index.html, the server tries to read the file /.htaccess, then /usr/-.htaccess, then /usr/local/.htaccess and then /usr/local/web/-.htaccess for directives, unless they have been disabled with "AllowOverride None".

Use AccessConfig and ResourceConfig only for backward-compatibility reasons.

- **AddModule**   **http_core**
Add Available Module to the List of Usable Modules
Syntax: AddModule *source-name* [*source-name* ...]
Example: AddModule mod_rewrite.c
Default: None
Since: Apache 1.2

Apache can have modules compiled in or loaded as DSO even if those modules are not actually activated. This directive can be used to enable those modules by adding them to the internal list of usable modules. By default, Apache has a preloaded list of activated modules. This list can be cleared with the ClearModuleList directive. Be aware that the argument *source-name* is really the file name of the primary source file of the module, (usually "mod_*name*.c").

Use a list of AddModule directives after a ClearModuleList directive to reconstruct the internal list of enabled modules in order to change their runtime processing priority.

- **AllowOverride**   **http_core**
Control Directives Allowed in Per-Directory Configuration Files
Syntax: AllowOverride *override* [*override* ...]
Example: AllowOverride AuthConfig FileInfo
Default: AllowOverride All
Since: Apache 1.0

Use `AllowOverride` to control what your users can re-configure on a local file system basis.

This directive controls which groups of other directives can be configured by per-directory configuration files (see `AccessFileName`). When the server finds an `.htaccess` file, it needs to know which directives declared in that file can override earlier access information. The argument *override* can be "none," in which case the server will not read the file at all. If it is *All*, the server will accept all directives, or one or more of the following: `AuthConfig` to allow the use of the authorization directives; `FileInfo` to allow the use of the directives controlling document types; `Indexes` to allow the use of the directives controlling directory indexing; `Limit` to allow the use of the directives controlling host access; and `Options` to allow the use of the directives controlling specific directory features (for instance, `Options` and `XBitHack` directives).

■ AuthName   http_core
Specify User Authentication Realm
Syntax: AuthName *realm*
Example: AuthName "Private Database"
Default: None
Since: Apache 1.0

This directive specifies the name of the authorization realm for a directory. This *realm* is given to the client so that the user knows which user name and password to send during HTTP *Basic Authentication*. The argument *realm* is a single argument; that is, if the realm name contains spaces, it must be enclosed in quotation marks. The directive must be accompanied by `AuthType` and `Require` directives, plus directives such as `AuthUserFile` and `AuthGroupFile`, to actually have any effects.

■ AuthType   http_core
Specify HTTP Authorization Type
Syntax: AuthType *type*
Example: AuthType Basic
Default: None
Since: Apache 1.0

This directive selects the *type* of HTTP user authentication for a directory. Only "Basic" (HTTP Basic Authentication) and "Digest" (HTTP Digest Authentication) are currently implemented for *type*. It must be accompanied by `AuthName` and `Require` directives, plus directives such as `AuthUserFile` and `AuthGroupFile`, to actually have any effects.

■ BindAddress   **http_core**
Bind to a TCP/IP Address (Deprecated)
Syntax: BindAddress *address*
Example: BindAddress 192.168.1.1
Default: BindAddress *
Since: Apache 1.0

Under UNIX, Apache can listen for connections to either every IP address of the server machine (the default) or just one IP address of the server machine. The argument *address* can be "*", a numerical IP address, or the name of a host with a unique IP address. If the value is "*", then Apache will listen for connections on every IP address; otherwise, it will listen on only the specified address.

The BindAddress is deprecated, use the superset directive Listen instead.

A maximum of one BindAddress directive can be used. To get more control over the addresses and ports to which Apache listens, use the Listen directive instead of BindAddress. This feature is generally used as an alternative method for supporting virtual hosts through multiple independent servers, instead of through <VirtualHost> sections.

■ ClearModuleList   **http_core**
Clear List of Usable Modules
Syntax: ClearModuleList
Example: ClearModuleList
Default: None
Since: Apache 1.2

Apache comes with a built-in list of activated and hence usable modules. This directive clears the list. It is assumed that the list will then be repopulated via the AddModule directive.

■ ContentDigest   **http_core**
Generation of Content-MD5 headers
Syntax: ContentDigest on|off
Example: ContentDigest on
Default: ContentDigest off
Since: Apache 1.1

This directive enables the generation of Content-MD5 headers as defined in RFC 1864 and RFC 2068, respectively. MD5 is an algorithm for computing a "message digest" (also known as a "fingerprint") of arbitrary-length data, with a high degree of confidence that any changes in the data will be reflected as changes in the message digest. The Content-MD5 header provides an end-to-end message integrity check of the HTTP response body. A proxy or client may check this header in an effort to detect accidental modification of the contents in transit.

■ CoreDumpDirectory　　　　　　　　　　　　**http_core**
Storage Location of Core Dumps
Syntax: CoreDumpDirectory *directory*
Example: CoreDumpDirectory /var/crash
Default: None
Since: Apache 1.3

This directive controls the directory to which Apache attempts to switch before dumping core files. The default is in the ServerRoot directory. This directory should not be writable by the user employed by the server, however, so core dumps are not normally written. Keep in mind that daemons start on most platforms under "root", so should never dump core files for security reasons.

■ DefaultType　　　　　　　　　　　　　　　**http_core**
Specify Default MIME Type for Documents
Syntax: DefaultType *mime-type*
Example: DefaultType application/octet-stream
Default: DefaultType text/html
Since: Apache 1.0

The server must inform the client of the content type of the document. In the event of a nondeterminable MIME type (no MIME type mappings apply), it therefore uses the value of this directive.

■ DocumentRoot　　　　　　　　　　　　　　**http_core**
Root Directory of Document Tree
Syntax: DocumentRoot *directory*
Example: DocumentRoot /home/www
Default: DocumentRoot htdocs
Since: Apache 1.0

This directive sets the *directory* from which Apache, by default, will serve documents. Unless matched by a directive like Alias or RewriteRule, the server appends the path from the requested URL to the *directory* argument to create a path to the document. To accommodate internal Apache logic, you should avoid trailing slashes in *directory*.

■ ErrorDocument　　　　　　　　　　　　　**http_core**
Set Alternative Response Document for HTTP Errors
Syntax: ErrorDocument *http-code action*
Example: ErrorDocument 302 /internal/302.html
Default: None
Since: Apache 1.0

In the event of a problem or error, Apache can be configured to do one of four things: (1) output a simple, hard-coded error message, (2) output a dynamic customized message, (3) redirect to a local URL to handle the problem, or (4) redirect to an external URL to handle the problem. The first option is the default. The other three options are configured using the ErrorDocument directive, which is followed by the HTTP response code *http-core* and a text message or URL *action*. Messages in this context consist of a quoted string for *action*. URLs for *action* can begin with a slash ("/") for local URLs or be fully qualified URLs that force an HTTP redirect.

■ ErrorLog   http_core
Server Log File for Errors
Syntax: ErrorLog *target*
Example: ErrorLog syslog:local
Default: ErrorLog logs/error_log
Since: Apache 1.0

This directive sets the target to which the server will log any errors it encounters. If *target* is a file name and does not begin with a slash ("/"), then it is assumed to be relative to ServerRoot. If it begins with a pipe ("|"), then it is assumed to be a command that spawns the errors. Alternatively, *target* can be "syslog:*facility*", which enables logging via syslog(3) if the system supports it. The default is to use syslog facility local7.

In case of any problems, always look into the log file specified via ErrorLog for details, first.

■ Group   http_core
Effective Group ID for Server Process
Syntax: Group *gid*
Example: Group nobody
Default: None
Since: Apache 1.0

This directive sets the (UNIX) group under which the server process will run and answer requests. To use this directive, the stand-alone server must be run initially as "root". The argument *gid* is either a group name or "#" followed by a numerical group ID. The use of this directive in <VirtualHost> requires a properly configured suEXEC wrapper. When used inside a <VirtualHost> in this manner, the directive affects only the group runs as CGI processes. All other types of requests are processed as the group specified in the main server.

HostnameLookups   http_core
Resolution of IP Addresses to Host Names
Syntax: HostnameLookups *type*
Example: HostnameLookups on
Default: HostnameLookups off
Since: Apache 1.1

To speed up runtime processing, you can use "HostnameLookups off" and "IdentityCheck off".

This directive specifies whether and how IP addresses of clients are re-solved to their corresponding host names via reverse DNS lookups, so that clients can be logged and passed to the CGI/SSI environment. The argument *type* can be "on" to enable full resolving, "off" to disable re-solving, or "double" to enable double-reverse DNS lookups.

In the latter approach, after a reverse lookup is performed, an ad-ditional forward lookup is carried out on that result. At least one of the IP addresses in the forward lookup must match the original address in a double-revers DNS lookup. Regardless of the setting, when mod_access is used for controlling access by host name, a double-reverse lookup will be always performed for security reasons.

IdentityCheck   http_core
Perform User Name Identification Lookups
Syntax: IdentityCheck *boolean*
Example: IdentityCheck on
Default: IdentityCheck off
Since: Apache 1.0

Spread your server configuration over multiple files with the help of the Include directive.

This directive supports RFC 1413-compliant user identification lookups, which can be used to log the remote user name for each connection. It works only if the remote host runs identd or something similar. The information is logged in the access log file and should not be trusted in any way except as part of rudimentary usage tracking. Note that this directive can create serious latency problems in accessing your server, because every request causes a lookup to be performed.

Include   http_core
Include Another Configuration File
Syntax: Include *file*
Example: Include vhost.conf
Default: None
Since: Apache 1.3

This directive allows the inclusion of another configuration file, given in the argument *file*. Use it with caution inside <Directory> sections, because the directive is applied to the surrounding context.

■ **KeepAlive** **http_core**
HTTP Keep-Alive Facility
Syntax: KeepAlive *boolean*
Example: KeepAlive on
Default: KeepAlive off
Since: Apache 1.1

This directive indicates whether the HTTP Keep-Alive facility is supported — that is, whether the client can establish persistent HTTP connections. Use of this directive is recommended, because it speeds up
request processing.

■ **KeepAliveTimeout** **http_core**
Set the Timeout for HTTP Keep-Alive Connections
Syntax: KeepAliveTimeout *seconds*
Example: KeepAliveTimeout 120
Default: KeepAliveTimeout 15
Since: Apache 1.1

This directive sets the number of seconds that the server will wait for a
subsequent request on a Keep-Alive connection before closing it. Once
a request has been received, the timeout value specified by the Timeout
directive applies.

■ **LimitRequestBody** **http_core**
Limit Maximum Size of Request Message Body
Syntax: LimitRequestBody *bytes*
Example: LimitRequestBody 512000
Default: LimitRequestBody 0
Since: Apache 1.3

This directive sets a maximum size (in bytes) for a request message
body. The *bytes* argument must be an integer between 0 (meaning unlimited) to 2,147,483,647 (2GB). If the client request exceeds the limit
on the allowed size of the HTTP request message body, the server will
return an error response instead of servicing the request. In this way,
the directive gives the server administrator greater control over abnormal client request behavior, which may help prevent some forms of
denial-of-service attacks.

Use the various
LimitRequestXXX
directives to restrict
incoming requests in
order to avoid Denial of
Service (DoS) attacks.

■ **LimitRequestFields** **http_core**
Limit Maximum Number of Request Fields
Syntax: LimitRequestFields *number*
Example: LimitRequestFields 20
Default: LimitRequestFields 100
Since: Apache 1.3

The directive specifies the maximum number of header fields that can appear in a request message. The *number* argument is an integer from 0 (meaning unlimited) to 32,767 (32KB). The directive allows a server administrator to modify the limit on the number of request header fields allowed in an HTTP request. This value should be larger than the number of fields that a normal client request might include. Use of this directive gives the server administrator greater control over abnormal client request behavior, which help prevent some forms of denial-of-service attacks.

■ LimitRequestFieldsize   **http_core**

Limit Maximum Size of Request Fields
Syntax: LimitRequestFieldsize *bytes*
Example: LimitRequestFieldsize 8190
Default: LimitRequestFieldsize 8190
Since: Apache 1.3

This directive specifies the maximum size of an HTTP request header field. The *bytes* argument is an integer from 0 (meaning unlimited) to 8,190 (slightly less than 8KB). The directive allows a server administrator to reduce the allowed size of an HTTP request header field below the normal input buffer size compiled with the server. This value should be large enough to hold any one header field from a normal client request. Use of this directive gives the server administrator greater control over abnormal client request behavior, which may help prevent some forms of denial-of-service attacks.

■ LimitRequestLine   **http_core**

Limit Maximum Size of Request Lines
Syntax: LimitRequestLine *bytes*
Example: LimitRequestLine 200
Default: LimitRequestLine 8190
Since: Apache 1.3

This directive specifies the maximum size of an HTTP request line. The bytes argument must be an integer size (in bytes) ranging from 0 to 8,190. Use of this directive allows the server administrator to reduce the allowed size of a client's HTTP request line below the normal input buffer size compiled with the server. Because the request line consists of the HTTP method, URL, and protocol version, the LimitRequest-Line directive places a restriction on the length of the URL allowed for a request on the server.

This value should be large enough to hold any of the resource names, including any information that might be passed in the query part of a

GET request. Use of this directive gives a server administrator greater control over abnormal client request behavior, which may help prevent some forms of Denial of Service attacks.

■ Listen   **http_core**
Listen to Multiple TCP/IP Addresses or Ports
Syntax: Listen [*ip-address*:]*port-number*
Example: Listen 443
Default: None
Since: Apache 1.1

This directive instructs the server to listen to more than one TCP/IP address or port; by default, it responds to requests on all IP interfaces, but only on the port given by the Port directive. The Listen directive can be used instead of BindAddress and Port. It tells the server to accept incoming requests on the specified port or address-and-port combination. If the first format (port number only) is used, the server listens to the given port on all interfaces, instead of the port given by the Port directive.

Use Listen to bind Apache to multiple TCP/IP addresses and/or ports for use with <VirtualHost> sections.

If an IP address is given as well as a port, the server will listen on the given port and interface. Note that a Port directive may also be required so that Apache-generated URLs that point to your server will continue to work. Multiple Listen directives may be used to specify a number of addresses and ports to which to listen. The server will respond to requests from any of the listed addresses and ports.

■ ListenBacklog   **http_core**
Maximum Length of the Queue of Pending Connections
Syntax: ListenBacklog *number*
Example: ListenBacklog 100
Default: ListenBacklog 512
Since: Apache 1.3

This directive specifies the maximum length of the queue of pending connections, as used by listen(2). Generally, no tuning is needed or desired, although on some systems it is desirable to increase tuning when under a TCP SYN flood attack. In many cases, the operating system will limit the backlog parameter to the listen(2) system call to a smaller number. This limitation varies from one operating system to the next. Also, note that many operating systems do not use the backlog exactly as specified, but instead use a number based on (but normally larger than) that set.

■ LockFile   **http_core**

Path to Lock File for Serialized Connection Accepts
Syntax: LockFile *path*
Example: LockFile /var/run/apache.lock
Default: LockFile logs/accept.lock
Since: Apache 1.2

The *path* is used when the server needs to lock the accept(2) call. This directive should normally be left at its default value. It might be changed if the log's directory is NFS-mounted, as the lock file must be stored on a local disk. The PID of the main server process is automatically appended to the file name. For security reasons, you should avoid putting this file in a world-writable directory, such as /var/tmp, because someone could launch a denial-of-service attack and prevent the server from starting by creating a lock file with the same name as the one the server will try to create.

■ LogLevel   **http_core**

Logging Level
Syntax: LogLevel *level*
Example: LogLevel warn
Default: LogLevel error
Since: Apache 1.3

Use "LogLevel error" on production web servers to reduce logging overhead.

This directive adjusts the verbosity of the messages recorded in the server's error logs (see the ErrorLog directive). The following levels are available, in order of decreasing significance: emerg (emergencies: system is unusable); alert (action must be taken immediately); crit (critical conditions); error (error conditions); warn (warning conditions); notice (normal but significant condition); info (informational messages); and debug (debugging messages). When a particular level is specified, messages from all other levels of higher significance will be reported as well.

■ MaxClients   **http_core**

Maximum Number of Clients
Syntax: MaxClients *number*
Example: MaxClients 128
Default: MaxClients 256
Since: Apache 1.0

This directive limits the number of simultaneous HTTP requests that can be supported; no more than this number of child server processes will be created. To configure more than 256 clients, one must edit the HARD_SERVER_LIMIT entry in httpd.h and recompile Apache. Any connection attempts that exceed the MaxClients limit will normally be queued in kernel space, up to a number based on the `ListenBacklog` directive. Once a child process is freed at the end of a different request, the queued connection will be serviced.

■ MaxKeepAliveRequests   http_core
Maximum Number of Keep-Alive Requests per Connection
Syntax: `MaxKeepAliveRequests` *number*
Example: `MaxKeepAliveRequests 20`
Default: `MaxKeepAliveRequests 100`
Since: Apache 1.2

This directive sets the maximum number of HTTP Keep-Alive requests allowed per established TCP/IP connection when `KeepAlive` is "on." Use 0 to specify an unlimited number of requests. Use high values to obtain maximum server performance.

■ MaxRequestsPerChild   http_core
Maximum Number of Requests per Server Child Process
Syntax: `MaxRequestsPerChild` *number*
Example: `MaxRequestsPerChild 10000`
Default: `MaxRequestsPerChild 0`
Since: Apache 1.0

This directive sets the maximum number of HTTP requests that an individual server child process can handle. After this number of requests is reached, the child process will die. If *number* is 0, then the process will never die automatically. For `KeepAlive` requests, only the first request counts toward this limit.

Use `MaxRequestsPerChild` to control the maximum number of HTTP requests that an individual server child process can handle.

■ MaxSpareServers   http_core
Maximum Number of Idle Server Child Processes
Syntax: `MaxSpareServers` *number*
Example: `MaxSpareServers 15`
Default: `MaxSpareServers 10`
Since: Apache 1.0

This directive sets the maximum number of idle server child processes. An idle process is one that is not currently handling a request. If more than *number* processes are idle, then the parent process will kill off the excess processes.

■ MinSpareServers   http_core
Minimum Number of Idle Server Child Processes
Syntax: `MinSpareServers` *number*
Example: `MinSpareServers 10`
Default: `MinSpareServers 5`
Since: Apache 1.0

This directive sets the minimum number of idle server child processes. An idle process is one that is not currently handling a request. If fewer than *number* processes are idle, then the parent process creates new children at a maximum rate of one per second.

▪ NameVirtualHost **http_core**

Declare a Name-based Virtual Host
Syntax: NameVirtualHost *host*[:*port*]
Example: NameVirtualHost 192.168.1.1
Default: None
Since: Apache 1.3

This directive is required if you want to configure name-based virtual hosts. Although *host* can be a host name or an IP address, it is recommended that you only use an IP address. With this directive, you specify the address to which your name-based virtual host names will resolve. If you have multiple name-based hosts on multiple addresses, repeat the directive for each address. Notice that the "main server" and any "_default_" servers will never be served for a request to a NameVirtualHost IP address.

Use NameVirtualHost in conjunction with <VirtualHost> sections to configure name-based (non IP-based) virtual hosting. But be aware that this does not work for the HTTPS protocol.

▪ Options **http_core**

Server Option Configuration
Syntax: Options [+|-]*option* [[+|-]*option* ...]
Example: Options +ExecCGI -MultiViews
Default: Options All
Since: Apache 1.0

This directive controls which server features are available in a particular directory. The *option* argument can be None, in which case none of the extra features is enabled. Alternatively, it can have one or more of the following values: All, for all options except MultiViews; ExecCGI, to permit the execution of CGI scripts; FollowSymLinks, to allow the server to follow symbolic links; Includes, to permit Server-Side Includes (SSI); IncludesNOEXEC, to permit SSI but not the SSI commands "#exec" and "#include"; Indexes, to enable the auto-generation of index pages if no DirectoryIndex file is found; MultiViews, to allow automatic content negotiation; and SymLinksIfOwnerMatch, to allow the server to follow only the symbolic links for which the target file or directory is owned by the same user ID as the link.

Normally, if multiple Options directives could apply to a directory, then the most specific one is taken by itself; the options are not merged. If all options on the Options directive are preceded by a "+" or "-" symbol, however, they are merged. Any options preceded by a "+" symbol are added to the options currently in force, and any options

Use the Options directive to restrict allowed features.

preceded by a "−" symbol are removed from the options currently in force.

■ **PidFile**   **http_core**
Process ID File
Syntax: PidFile *file*
Example: PidFile /var/run/apache.pid
Default: PidFile logs/httpd.pid
Since: Apache 1.0

This directive sets the *file* to which the server records the process ID of the daemon (actually, the PID of the parent server process). If the *file* argument does not begin with a slash (/), then it is assumed to be relative to ServerRoot. The PidFile is used only in stand-alone mode. It is often desirable to send a signal to the server, so that it closes and then reopens its ErrorLog and TransferLog, and rereads its configuration files. This task is accomplished by sending a SIGHUP signal to the process ID listed in the PidFile.

■ **Port**   **http_core**
Canonical Port Number
Syntax: Port *number*
Example: Port 8080
Default: Port 80
Since: Apache 1.0

This directive configures the canonical port of the server (in addition to the ServerName directive, which configures the canonical host name). A Port setting never affects the ports on which a <VirtualHost> actually responds; the <VirtualHost> and Listen directives are used for that purpose. The *number* argument is a numerical value ranging from 0 to 65535. The standard port for the HTTP protocol is 80. All ports numbered below 1024 are reserved for system use under UNIX. That is, regular (nonprivileged) users cannot use them; instead, they can use only higher port numbers. To use such low-numbered ports, one must start the server from the "root" account.

Keep in mind that Port never affects the ports on which a <VirtualHost> actually responds; the <VirtualHost> and Listen directives are used for that purpose.

■ **RLimitCPU**   **http_core**
Resource Limit on CPU Usage
Syntax: RLimitCPU *soft-seconds* [*hard-seconds*]
Example: RLimitCPU 60 120
Default: None
Since: Apache 1.2

This directive sets the soft and hard limits for maximum CPU usage of a process in seconds. It takes one or two parameters. The first parameter, *soft-seconds*, sets the soft resource limit for all processes. The second parameter, *hard-seconds*, sets the maximum resource limit. Either parameter can be a number, or "max", which indicates to the server that the limit should match the maximum allowed by the operating system configuration. Raising the maximum resource limit requires the server to be running as the user "root," or in the initial start-up phase.

RLimitMEM   http_core
Resource Limit on Memory Usage
Syntax: RLimitMEM *soft-bytes* [*hard-bytes*]
Example: RLimitMEM 1048576 2097152
Default: None
Since: Apache 1.2

Use the various
RLimitXXX to restrict
the runtime resource
limits of server
processes.

This directive sets the soft and hard limits for maximum memory usage of a process in bytes. It takes one or two parameters. The first parameter sets the soft resource limit for all processes. The second parameter sets the maximum resource limit. Either parameter can be a number, or "max", which indicates to the server that the limit should match the maximum allowed by the operating system configuration. Raising the maximum resource limit requires the server to be running as the user "root" or in the initial start-up phase.

RLimitNPROC   http_core
Resource Limit on Number of Processes
Syntax: RLimitNPROC *soft-processes* [*hard-processes*]
Example: RLimitNPROC
Default: None
Since: Apache 1.2

This directive sets the soft and hard limits for the maximum number of processes per user or user ID (UID). It takes one or two parameters. The first parameter sets the soft resource limit for all processes. The second parameter sets the maximum resource limit. Either parameter can be a number, or "max", which indicates to the server that the limit should match the maximum allowed by the operating system configuration. Raising the maximum resource limit requires the server to be running as "root" or in the initial start-up phase. If CGI processes are not running under UIDs other than the web server UID, this directive will limit the number of processes that the server itself can create. This situation will be indicated by "cannot fork" messages in the error log file.

▪ Require   http_core
Require User and Group Authentication
Syntax: Require *type* [*uid-or-gid* [...]]
Example: Require group friends
Default: None
Since: Apache 1.0

This directive selects which authenticated users or groups may access
a protected directory. The following syntax variants are allowed: "require user *uid* [*uid* ...]", which means that only the named users can
access the directory; "require group *gid* [*gid* ...]", which means that
only users in the named groups can access the directory; and "require
valid-user", which means that all valid users can access the directory.
If this directive appears in a <Limit> section, then it restricts access
to the named HTTP methods; otherwise, it restricts access for all methods. Require must be accompanied by AuthName and AuthType directives, as well as directives such as AuthUserFile and AuthGroupFile
(to define users and groups), to work correctly.

▪ ResourceConfig   http_core
Extra Resource Configuration File (Deprecated)
Syntax: ResourceConfig *file*
Example: ResourceConfig /dev/null
Default: ResourceConfig conf/srm.conf
Since: Apache 1.0

The server reads the specified *file* for more directives after reading the
httpd.conf file. The argument *file* is relative to the ServerRoot. Historically, this file contained most of the directives, except for the server
configuration directives and the Directory sections in NCSA httpd
(the ancestor of Apache). Since the early Apache days, however, it has
been allowed to contain any server directives in the server configuration context. This directive has been officially deprecated since Apache
1.3 and is typically disabled using "ResourceConfig /dev/null".

Use "Satisfy any" if
access to a particular
area is being allowed
either by user
name/password or
client host address.

▪ Satisfy   http_core
Special Access Policy Under the Allow and Require Directives
Syntax: Satisfy *type*
Example: Satisfy any
Default: Satisfy all
Since: Apache 1.2

This directive dictates a special access policy if both the Allow and
Require directives are used. The parameter *type* can be either "all"
or "any". The Satisfy directive is useful only if access to a particular area is being restricted by both user name/password (via Require)

and client host address (via `Allow`). In this case, the default behavior ("all") is to require that the client pass the address access restriction *and* enter a valid user name and password. Under "any" the client will be granted access if it either passes the host restriction *or* enters a valid user name/password. The goal is intended to password-restrict an area, while letting in clients from particular addresses without prompting them for a password.

■ ScoreBoardFile   **http_core**
Runtime Process Management Information File
Syntax: `ScoreBoardFile file`
Example: `ScoreBoardFile /var/run/apache.score`
Default: `ScoreBoardFile logs/apache_status`
Since: Apache 1.0

On some architectures, this directive is required to specify a file that the server will use to communicate between its children and the parent so as to manage the process pool.

■ SendBufferSize   **http_core**
TCP/IP Send Buffer Size
Syntax: `SendBufferSize bytes`
Example: `SendBufferSize 131072`
Default: `None`
Since: Apache 1.2

This directive forces the server to set the TCP/IP send buffer size to the number of *bytes* specified. It allows you to increase the standard operating system defaults on high-speed, high-latency network links. The default value for *bytes* depends on the particular operating system.

■ ServerAdmin   **http_core**
E-Mail Address of the Server Administrator
Syntax: `ServerAdmin account@fqdn`
Example: `ServerAdmin webmaster@foo.bar.dom`
Default: `None`
Since: Apache 1.0

This directive sets the e-mail address that the server includes in error messages returned to the client.

- ### ServerAlias   http_core
  Alternative Server Names
  Syntax: `ServerAlias host [host ...]`
  Example: `ServerAlias www.foo.dom foo.dom`
  Default: `None`
  Since: Apache 1.1

  This directive sets the alternative host names for a server, for use with name-based virtual hosts (that is, the mechanism behind the HTTP Host header).

  Configure with `ServerAlias` the alternative host names of your web server.

- ### ServerName   http_core
  Canonical Server Host Name
  Syntax: `ServerName host`
  Example: `ServerName www.foo.dom`
  Default: `None`
  Since: Apache 1.0

  This directive sets the canonical host name of the server. It is used mainly to create redirection URLs. If the host name is not specified, then the server attempts to deduce it from its own IP address; this process may not work reliably or may not return the preferred host name, however.

- ### ServerPath   http_core
  Explicit Server Selection Path Name
  Syntax: `ServerPath url-path`
  Example: `ServerPath`
  Default: `None`
  Since: Apache 1.1

  This directive sets the legacy URL path name for a host to *url-path*, for use with name-based virtual hosts and older browsers that do not support (or send) the HTTP Host header field. Such browsers would not be able to access a name-based virtual host. With this directive, they can use `http://www.domain.dom/`*url-path*`/` as a workaround to access the web site `http://www.domain.dom/`.

  `ServerPath` is for poor man's name-based virtual hosting.

- ### ServerRoot   http_core
  Server Root Directory
  Syntax: `ServerRoot path`
  Example: `ServerRoot /sw/pkg/apache`
  Default: `ServerRoot /usr/local/apache`
  Since: Apache 1.0

  This directive sets the root directory in which the server resides. Typically, it contains the subdirectories `conf/` and `logs/`. Relative paths for other configuration files are taken as relative to this directory. This directive can also be overridden from the command line via the -d option.

■ ServerSignature

http_core

Control Server Signature
Syntax: ServerSignature *type*
Example: ServerSignature on
Default: ServerSignature off
Since: Apache 1.3

This directive allows the configuration of a trailing footer line under server-generated documents (error messages, mod_proxy ftp directory listings, mod_info output, and so on. In a chain of proxies, the user often cannot tell which of the chained servers actually produced a returned error message; a footer line overcomes this problem. A *type* argument of "off", which is the default, suppresses the error line. The value "on" adds a line with the server version number and ServerName of the serving virtual host. The value "email" also creates a "mailto:" reference to the ServerAdmin of the referenced document.

■ ServerTokens

http_core

Control Tokens Displayed in HTTP Server Header Field
Syntax: ServerTokens *type*
Example: ServerTokens min
Default: ServerTokens full
Since: Apache 1.3

Use "ServerTokens min" if you are paranoid when it comes to security.

This directive controls whether the HTTP Server response header field, which is sent back to clients, includes a description of the generic operating system type of the server (if *type* is "os") as well as information about compiled-in modules (if *type* is "full"). With a *type* of "min", only the server version is included. This setting applies to the entire server, and it cannot be enabled or disabled on a per-virtual-host basis.

■ ServerType

http_core

Execution Environment of the Server
Syntax: ServerType *type*
Example: ServerType inetd
Default: ServerType standalone
Since: Apache 1.0

This directive sets how the system will execute the server. The *type* argument is either "inetd", in which case the server will run from the system process inetd (the command to start the server is added to /etc/inetd.conf), or "standalone", in which case the server will run as a stand-alone daemon process (the command to start the server is added to the system start-up scripts). The inetd type is deprecated and should be avoided, because it is an inefficient execution mode and because Apache has dropped real support for this mode.

■ StartServers   http_core
Number of Child Processes to Launch at Server Start-up
Syntax: StartServers *number*
Example: StartServers 20
Default: StartServers 5
Since: Apache 1.0

This directive sets the *number* of server child processes created during server start-up. Because the number of processes is dynamically controlled based on the load, it is rarely necessary to adjust this parameter.

Do not use "ServerType inetd" anymore — it is no longer supported and is even slightly broken.

■ Timeout   http_core
General Processing Timeout Duration
Syntax: Timeout *seconds*
Example: Timeout 60
Default: Timeout 300
Since: Apache 1.0

This directive defines the amount of time Apache will wait on three occasions: (1) the total amount of time it takes to receive an HTTP GET request; (2) the amount of time between receipt of TCP packets on a POST or PUT request; (3) the amount of time between acknowledgments on transmissions of TCP packets in responses.

Use a reasonable Timeout directive to prevent Denial of Service (DoS) attacks to your web server.

■ UseCanonicalName   http_core
Control the Use of Canonical Server Name
Syntax: UseCanonicalName *type*
Example: UseCanonicalName off
Default: UseCononicalName on
Since: Apache 1.3

In many situations, the server must construct a self-referential URL — that is, a URL that refers back to the same server. With *type* set to "on", the server will use the ServerName and Port directives to construct a canonical name. This name is then used in all self-referential URLs, as well as for the values of SERVER_NAME and SERVER_PORT in the SSI/CGI environment.

With *type* set to "off", the server will form self-referential URLs using the host name and port supplied by the client in the HTTP Host header field, if any is supplied (otherwise, it will use the canonical name). These values are the same as those used to implement name-based virtual hosts, and they are available with the same clients. The SSI/CGI variables SERVER_NAME and SERVER_PORT will be constructed from the client-supplied values as well.

There is a third option in setting *type*: "dns", which is intended for use with mass IP-based virtual hosting to support ancient clients that do not provide an HTTP Host header field. With this option, the server performs a reverse DNS lookup on the server IP address to which the client connected to work out self-referential URLs.

■ **User**   **http_core**
Effective User ID for Server Processes
Syntax: User *uid*
Example: User nobody
Default: User #-1
Since: Apache 1.0

Always specify a nonprivileged user with the User directive and never the "root" user.

This directive sets the user ID to *uid*; the server will answer requests from this ID. To use this directive, the stand-alone server must be run initially as the user "root." The *uid* argument can be either a real user name (to refer to the given user by name), or "#" followed by a numerical user ID (to refer to a user by number). For security reasons, the user should have no privileges that allow him or her to access files that are not intended to be visible to the outside world. Similarly, the user should not be able to execute code that is not meant for HTTP requests.

Note that the use of this directive in <VirtualHost> requires a properly configured suEXEC wrapper. When used inside a <VirtualHost> in this manner, this directive affects only the user associated with CGIs requests. Non-CGI requests continue to be processed with the user specified in the main User directive.

mod_so
Dynamic Shared Object (DSO) Bootstrapping

■ **LoadFile**   **mod_so**
Load DSO Files into Apache's Address Space
Syntax: LoadFile *file* [*file* ...]
Example: LoadFile /usr/lib/libdb.so /lib/libm.so
Default: None
Since: Apache 1.0

This directive loads one or more DSO object or library files when the server is started (or restarted). No special handling of these DSOs occurs; instead, mod_so just loads them but does not work with them explicitly. This directive is useful for bootstrap loading additional code that may be required for some (DSO-based) Apache modules to work. The argument *file* is either an absolute path or relative to ServerRoot.

Use LoadFile to load additional shared libraries if object file format does not know about dependencies between DSOs.

■ LoadModule   mod_so

Load DSO Apache Module into Apache's Address Space
Syntax: LoadModule *module-handle module-file*
Example: LoadModule env_module libexec/mod_env.so
Default: None
Since: Apache 1.0

This directive loads a DSO-based Apache module *module-file*, looks up its entry point through the object file symbol *module-handle*, and adds this module to Apache's internal list of known modules. The argument *module-handle* is the name of the external variable of type "module" in the module's source code. The argument *module-file* is either an absolute path or relative to ServerRoot.

Use LoadModule to extend your server functionality without having to recompile Apache from source.

4.3.2   URL Mapping

mod_alias
Simple URL Translation and Redirection

■ Alias   mod_alias

Map a URL Prefix to a File Name Prefix
Syntax: Alias *url-prefix fs-prefix*
Example: Alias /image /www/image
Default: None
Since: Apache 1.0

This directive allows documents to be stored in the local file system in a location other than under DocumentRoot. URLs whose path begins with *url-prefix* will be mapped to local files whose path begins with *fs-prefix*. For instance, in the preceding example, a request for http://thisserver/image/foo/bar.gif would cause the server to return the file /www/image/foo/bar.gif.

Use Alias for prefix-based URL manipulations and AliasMatch if you need more flexibility.

▪ AliasMatch   mod_alias
Map a URL to a File Name Path via Regular Expression Match
Syntax: AliasMatch *url-pattern fs-path*
Example: AliasMatch ↑(.+\.(gif))$ /www/$2/$1
Default: None
Since: Apache 1.3

This directive is equivalent to Alias, but uses standard regular expressions, instead of simple prefix matching. The supplied regular expression *url-pattern* is compared with the request URL. If it matches, the server will substitute any matches found in parentheses in *fs-path* into the given string and use it as a file system path. For instance, in the preceding example, a request for http://host/foo/bar.gif would cause the server to return the file /www/gif/bar.gif.

▪ Redirect   mod_alias
Redirect URL Prefix to External Resource
Syntax: Redirect [*status*] *url-prefix redirect-prefix*
Example: Redirect /image http://image.foo.dom/
Default: None
Since: Apache 1.0

This directive is similar to Alias in that all URLs starting with *url-prefix* use *redirect-prefix* as a substitution, except that *redirect-prefix* must be an absolute URL. The resulting HTTP redirect is sent back to the client. The optional *status* argument can be used to return particular HTTP status codes: permanent returns a permanent redirect status (301) indicating that the resource has moved permanently; temp returns a temporary redirect status (302, the default); seeother returns a status (303) indicating that the resource has been replaced; or gone returns a status (410) indicating that the resource has been permanently removed.

When this status is used, the *redirect-prefix* argument should be omitted. Other status codes can be returned by giving the numeric status code as the value of *status*. If the status is between 300 and 399, the *redirect-prefix* argument must be present; otherwise, omit it.

▪ RedirectMatch   mod_alias
Redirect URL via Regular Expression Match
Syntax: RedirectMatch [*status*] *url-pattern* [*redirect-url*]
Example: RedirectMatch ↑/(a.+)$ http://foo.dom/$1
Default: None
Since: Apache 1.3

This directive is similar to `AliasMatch`, except that the result is an absolute URL to an external resource instead of a local file system path.

■ RedirectPermanent   mod_alias
Redirect URL Permanently
Syntax: RedirectPermanent ***url-prefix external-resource***
Example: RedirectPermanent /image http://foo.dom/
Default: None
Since: Apache 1.2

This directive exists for backward-compatibility reasons only. It is equivalent to using `Redirect` with a ***status*** argument of permanent.

■ RedirectTemp   mod_alias
Redirect URL Temporarily
Syntax: RedirectTemp ***url-prefix external-resource***
Example: RedirectTemp /image http://foo.dom/image
Default: None
Since: Apache 1.2

This directive exists for backward-compatibility reasons only. It is equivalent to using `Redirect` with a ***status*** argument of temp.

■ ScriptAlias   mod_alias
Map a URL Prefix to a Script Prefix
Syntax: ScriptAlias ***url-prefix fs-prefix***
Example: ScriptAlias /cgi-bin /www/cgi-bin
Default: None
Since: Apache 1.0

This directive has the same behavior and syntax as the `Alias` directive, but it also marks the target directory as containing CGI scripts. URLs whose path begins with ***url-prefix*** will be mapped to scripts that begin with ***fs-prefix***.

`ScriptAlias` is like a combination of `Alias` and "`Options +ExecCGI`".

■ ScriptAliasMatch   mod_alias
Map a URL to a Script Path via Regular Expression Match
Syntax: ScriptAliasMatch ***url-pattern fs-path***
Example: ScriptAliasMatch
Default: None
Since: Apache 1.3

This directive is equivalent to `ScriptAlias`, but uses standard regular expressions instead of simple prefix matching. The supplied regular expression ***url-pattern*** is compared with the URL. If it matches, the server will substitute any matches in parentheses in *fs-path* into the given string and use it as a script file name.

mod_rewrite
Advanced URL Translation and Redirection

■ **RewriteEngine**   **mod_rewrite**
Rewrite Engine Operation Switch
Syntax: RewriteEngine on|off
Example: RewriteEngine on
Default: RewriteEngine off
Since: Apache 1.2

This directive enables or disables the runtime rewriting engine. If it is set to off, then mod_rewrite does no runtime processing. Use this directive to disable mod_rewrite instead of commenting out all Rewrite-Rule directives. By default, rewrite configurations are not inherited. Thus you need a RewriteEngine directive to switch this configuration on for each virtual host in which you wish to use it.

■ **RewriteOptions**   **mod_rewrite**
Rewrite Engine Options
Syntax: RewriteOptions *option* [*option* ...]
Example: RewriteOptions inherit
Default: None
Since: Apache 1.2

This directive offers some special options for the current per-server or per-directory configuration of mod_rewrite. Currently, only one *option* is implemented: inherit. It forces the current configuration to inherit the configuration of the parent. In per-virtual-server context, this option means that the RewriteMap, RewriteCond, and RewriteRule of the main server are inherited. In per-directory context, it means that the RewriteCond and RewriteRule of the parent directory's .htaccess configuration are inherited.

■ **RewriteLog**   **mod_rewrite**
Rewrite Engine Logging Target
Syntax: RewriteLog *file*
Example: RewriteLog logs/rewrite_log
Default: None
Since: Apache 1.2

This directive sets the *file* of the dedicated rewriting engine log file. It should appear where it cannot be used for symbolic link attacks on a real server (that is, a location where only "root" can write). If the file name does not begin with a slash ("/"), then it is assumed to be relative to the *server root*. If *file* begins with a bar ("|"), then the following string is assumed to be a file path to an executable program to which a reliable pipe can be established.

■ RewriteLogLevel   mod_rewrite
Rewrite Engine Logging Level
Syntax: RewriteLogLevel *level*
Example: RewriteLogLevel 3
Default: RewriteLogLevel 0
Since: Apache 1.2

This directive sets the verbosity degree of the rewriting engine log file ($\rightarrow$ RewriteLog). The *level* argument is a number between 0 and 9, where 0 disables the log file writing and 9 outputs even debugging information.

Use "RewriteLogLevel 9" to debug your URL manipulations if they do not work.

■ RewriteLock   mod_rewrite
Rewrite Engine Mutual Exclusion Lock
Syntax: RewriteLock *file*
Example: RewriteLock logs/rewrite_lock
Default: None
Since: Apache 1.3

This directive sets the file name for a synchronization mutual exclusion lock *file* that mod_rewrite needs to communicate with RewriteMap programs. Set *file* to a local path (not on a NFS-mounted device) when you want to use a rewriting map program. This directive is not required for other types of rewriting maps.

■ RewriteMap   mod_rewrite
Rewrite Map
Syntax: RewriteMap *map-name map-type*:*map-source*
Example: RewriteMap user-to-host txt:conf/u2h
Default: None
Since: Apache 1.2

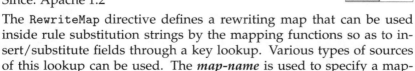

The RewriteMap directive defines a rewriting map that can be used inside rule substitution strings by the mapping functions so as to insert/substitute fields through a key lookup. Various types of sources of this lookup can be used. The *map-name* is used to specify a mapping function for the substitution strings of a rewriting rule via ${*map-name*:*lookup-key*[*default-value*]} constructs. When such a construct oc-

Use RewriteMap if you need more complex URL manipulations.

curs, the map *map-name* is consulted and the key *lookup-key* is looked up. If the key is found, the looked-up value is substituted for the construct. If the key is not found, then the *default-value* or the empty string (if no *default-value* was specified) is used.

The following combinations for *map-type* and *map-source* can be used: Standard Plain Text (*map-type*: `txt`, *map-source*: UNIX file path to valid regular text file); Randomized Plain Text (*map-type*: `rnd`, *map-source*: UNIX file path to valid regular text file); Hash File (*map-type*: `dbm`, *map-source*: UNIX file system path to valid regular NDBM file); Internal Function (*map-type*: `int`, *map-source*: `toupper`, `tolower`, `escape`, or `unescape`); and External Rewriting Program (*map-type*: `prg`, *map-source*: UNIX file system path to valid regular executable).

The `RewriteMap` directive can occur multiple times. Keep in mind that while you cannot *declare* a rewriting map in a per-directory context, it is possible to *use* it in a per-directory context.

■ RewriteBase   mod_rewrite

Rewrite URL Base
Syntax: RewriteBase *url*
Example: RewriteBase /~foo/bar/
Default: None
Since: Apache 1.2

This directive explicitly sets the base URL for per-directory rewriting. It is useful because `RewriteRule` can be used in per-directory configuration files where it will act locally. That is, the local directory prefix is stripped at this stage of processing and your rewriting rules act only on the remainder. The URL is added automatically at the end. Thus, when a substitution occurs for a new URL, mod_rewrite reinjects the URL into the server processing. To carry out this task, it needs to know the corresponding URL prefix or URL base. By default, the URL prefix is the corresponding file path itself. At most web sites, however, URLs are *not* directly related to physical file name paths, so this assumption will usually be wrong! In such a case, you must use the `RewriteBase` directive to specify the correct URL prefix.

On redirects help Apache to know your URL by using `RewriteBase` in ".htaccess" files.

■ RewriteCond   mod_rewrite

Rewrite Condition
Syntax: RewriteCond *test-string pattern* [[*flag*,...]]
Example: RewriteCond %{HTTP_HOST} ↑.+\.foo\.dom$
Default: None
Since: Apache 1.2

This directive defines a rewriting rule condition. A `RewriteRule` directive can be preceded with one or more `RewriteCond` directives. The

RewriteRule is then used only if its pattern matches the current state of the URL *and* the preceding conditions apply. The *test-string* can contain the following (to be expanded) constructs in addition to plain text: rule pattern back-references ($*N*, *N* = 1,2,...), condition pattern back-references (%*N*, *N* = 1,2,...), or server variables (%{*NAME*}). The *pattern* is the condition pattern — that is, a regular expression that is applied to the instance of the *test-string*. In other words, *test-string* is evaluated and then compared with *pattern*. Special *pattern*s and additional *flags* also exist. For more details, see the mod_rewrite online documentation.

Use one or more RewriteCond directives in conjunction with a RewriteRule if you need complex conditional URL manipulations.

▣ RewriteRule   mod_rewrite
Rewrite Rule

Syntax: RewriteRule *url-pattern url-new* [[*flag*, . . .]]
Example: RewriteRule ↑/foo/(.*)$ /bar/$1 [R,L]
Default: None
Since: Apache 1.2

This directive is the real rewriting workhorse. It can occur more than once. Each directive then defines a single rewriting rule. The definition order of these rules is important, because it is used when applying the rules at runtime. The *url-pattern* is a regular expression that is applied to the current URL, where "current" means at the time when this rule is applied. The current URL may not be the original requested URL, because any number of previous rules could have already matched and altered it.

RewriteRule directives configure an ordered list of URL rewriting rules.

The *url-new* argument is the string that is substituted for the original URL matched by the *url-pattern*. Beside plain text, you can use back-references ($*N*) to the *url-pattern*, back- references (%*N*) to the last matched RewriteCond pattern, server variables such as RewriteCond test strings (%{*NAME*}), and mapping function calls (${*map-name:lookup-key|default-value*}) for this argument.

In addition, you can set special flags for *url-new* by appending one or more *flag* arguments. The flag argument is actually a comma-separated list of the following flags: redirect (or R) to force an HTTP redirect; forbidden (or F) to forbid access; gone (or G) to eliminate the URL; proxy (or P) to pass the URL to mod_proxy; last (or L) to stop processing; next (or N) to start the next round of processing; chain (or C) to chain the current rule with the following one; type (or T) to force a particular MIME type; nosubreq (or NS) to ensure that the rule applies only if no internal sub-request is performed; nocase (or NC) to force the URL matching to be case-insensitive; qsappend (or QSA) to append a query string part in *url-new* to the existing one instead of replacing it; passthrough (or PT) to pass the rewritten URL through to other

Apache modules; skip (or S) to skip the next rule; and env (or E) to set an environment variable. For more details, see the mod_rewrite online documentation.

mod_userdir
URL Selection by User Names

■ **UserDir**   **mod_userdir**
Configure
Syntax: UserDir *pattern* [...]
Example: UserDir /home/*/public_html/
Default: None
Since: Apache 1.0

The UserDir directive controls how Apache finds the personal home pages of your users.

This directive configures URL-to-file system mappings for the home directory of users. Apache uses this directive if it receives a request for a document for a user (URLs starting with "/˜*username*"); UserDir can then find the documents inside the home directory of *username*. The *pattern* argument is usually either the name of a directory path or a directory pattern.

If *pattern* does not start with a slash ("/"), then mod_userdir assumes that it is the subdirectory inside the user's home directory containing the desired documents. If *pattern* starts with a slash, two other situations are possible. First, *pattern* contains a wildcard (an asterisk "*"), then the asterisk is replaced by *username* and the result is treated as the prefix for the user's documents root. Second, *userdir* may be appended to the pattern and the result treated as the prefix for the user's documents root.

Several special variants of *pattern* exist as well. If *pattern* is "disabled *username1 username2* ...," then no URL translations of the specified user names are made. If *pattern* is just "disabled," *all* URL translations are turned off except those explicitly named with the "enabled" keyword. If *pattern* is "enabled *username1 username2* ...," then URL translations for the specified user names are allowed.

mod_imap
URL Selection by Image Map Coordinates

■ **ImapBase**   **mod_imap**
Default Base URL for Image Maps
Syntax: ImapBase *base*
Example: ImapBase http://www.foo.dom/maps
Default: ImapBase http://servername/
Since: Apache 1.1

This directive sets the default URL base used in image map files. Its value is overridden by a Base directive within the image map file. The *base* argument can be either map (the base is specified in the image map file), referer (the base is forced by the client with the HTTP Referer header field), or a fully qualified URL.

The mod_imap directives are for processing old server-side image maps only. Nowadays you usually want to stick with client-side image maps instead.

■ ImapDefault   mod_imap
Default Action for Image Maps
Syntax: ImapDefault *action*
Example: ImapDefault error
Default: ImapDefault nocontent
Since: Apache 1.1

This directive sets the default action used in the image map files. Its value may be overridden by a default directive within the image map file. If no such default directive is present, the default *action* is nocontent, which means that the client receives a 204 ("No Content") HTTP response. In this case, the client should continue to display the original page. Alternatively, one can set the following actions: "error" to display a server error page; "menu" to display a menu page (as controlled by ImapMenu) with hyperlinks to possible actions; "referer" to redirect back to the origin URL; or a fully qualified URL to force an HTTP redirection to a particular URL.

■ ImapMenu   mod_imap
Type of Generated Menu for Image Maps
Syntax: ImapMenu *type*
Example: ImapMenu none
Default: ImapMenu formatted
Since: Apache 1.1

This directive determines the action taken if an image map file is called without valid coordinates. With a *type* of "none," no menu is generated and the default action is performed; "formatted" displays a well-formatted menu derived from the image map file; "semiformatted" displays a minimally formatted menu derived from the image map file; and "unformatted" treats the image map file as HTML instead of plaintext and ignores extra formatting.

mod_speling
URL Spelling Correction

■ CheckSpelling   mod_speling
Spelling Module Operation Switch
Syntax: CheckSpelling on|off
Example: CheckSpelling on
Default: CheckSpelling off
Since: Apache 1.3

Use "CheckSpelling on" if you have lots of users who keep thinking URLs are case-insensitive.

This directive toggles the operation of mod_speling. When its operation is turned on, incorrectly capitalized and misspelled URLs in requests are fixed as if by magic. Keep in mind that the directory scan that is necessary for the spelling correction will affect the server's performance when many spelling corrections must be performed at the same time.

4.3.3   Access Control

mod_access
Host- and Network-Based Access Control

■ Allow   mod_access
Allow Access by Host Name or IP Address
Syntax: Allow from *source* [from *source* ...]
Example: Allow from .foo.dom
Default: None
Since: Apache 1.0

This directive specifies which hosts can access a given directory. The argument *source* can be one of the following: "all" to allow access from all hosts; a (partial) domain name to allow access from hosts whose names match, or end in, the specified string; a full IP address (such as "192.168.1.2") to allow access from only this particular IP address; a partial IP address (first one to three bytes of an IP address, such as "192.168.1") for subnet access restriction; a network/net mask pair (such as "192.168.0.0/255.255.0.0") for more fine-grained subnet restriction; or a network/CIDR specification (such as "192.168.0.0/16") for more fine-grained subnet restriction.

In addition, *source* can be of the form "env=*variable*", which controls access to a directory through the existence (or nonexistence) of an environment variable named *variable*. Notice that this directive always compares whole components; hence "bar.edu" would not match "foo-bar.edu".

■ Deny   mod_access

Deny Access by Host Name or IP Address

Syntax: Deny from *source* [from *source* ...]

Example: Deny from all

Default: None

Since: Apache 1.0

This directive specifies which hosts cannot access a given directory. The argument *source* can be one of the following: "all" to deny access from all hosts; a (partial) domain name to deny access from hosts whose names match, or end in, the specified string; a full IP address (such as "192.168.1.2") to deny access from only this particular IP address; a partial IP address (first one to three bytes of an IP address, such as "192.168.1") for subnet access restriction; a network/net mask pair (such as "192.168.0.0/255.255.0.0") for more fine-grained subnet restriction; or a network/CIDR specification (such as "192.168.0.0/16") for more fine-grained subnet restriction.

Use the Allow, Deny, and Order directives to control access by host or network.

In addition, *source* can be of the form "env=*variable*", which controls access to a directory through the existence (or nonexistence) of an environment variable named *variable*. Notice that this directive always compares whole components; hence "bar.edu" would not match "foo-bar.edu".

■ Order   mod_access

Order in Which Allow and Deny Directives Are Evaluated

Syntax: Order *type*

Example: Order allow,deny

Default: Order deny,allow

Since: Apache 1.0

This directive controls the order in which Allow and Deny directives are evaluated. The *type* argument can be one of the following: "deny,allow", which means that the Deny directives are evaluated before the Allow directives (the initial state is to allow); "allow,deny," which means that the Allow directives are evaluated before the Deny directives (the initial state is to deny); or "mutual-failure," which means that only those hosts that appear on the Allow list but not on the Deny list are granted access (the initial state is irrelevant). In all cases, *every* Allow and Deny statement is evaluated. That is, no "short-circuiting" takes place.

4.3.4   User Authentication

mod_auth
User Authentication by User Name/Password

■ **AuthAuthoritative**   **mod_auth**
Allow Access Control to Be Passed to Lower-Level Modules
Syntax: `AuthAuthoritative on|off`
Example: `AuthAuthoritative off`
Default: `AuthAuthoritative on`
Since: Apache 1.2

Setting this directive explicitly to "`off`" permits both authentication
and authorization to be passed to lower-level modules (as defined in
the `Configuration` and `modules.c` files at buildtime) if no user ID or
rule matches the supplied user ID. If a user ID or rule is specified,
the usual password and access checks are applied and a failure gives
an "`Authorization Required`" reply. The `AuthAuthoritative` directive is typically used in conjunction with a database module, such as
`mod_auth_db` or `mod_auth_dbm`. These modules supply the bulk of the
user credential checking, although a few administrator-related accesses
may fall through to a lower level with a well-protected `AuthUserFile`.

■ **AuthGroupFile**   **mod_auth**
Textual File of Authentication Groups
Syntax: `AuthGroupFile` *filename*
Example: `AuthGroupFile etc/groups`
Default: `None`
Since: Apache 1.0

This directive sets the name of a textual file containing the list of user
groups for user authentication. The argument *filename* consists of the
path to the group file. If not an absolute path name, it is treated as
being relative to the `ServerRoot`. Each line of the group file contains a
group name followed by a colon, followed by the member user names
separated by spaces (for example, "`foo:  bar quux`").

■ **AuthUserFile**   **mod_auth**
Textual File of Authentication Users
Syntax: `AuthUserFile` *filename*
Example: `AuthUserFile etc/passwd`
Default: `None`
Since: Apache 1.0

This directive sets the name of a textual file containing the list of users and passwords for user authentication. The argument *filename* consists of the path to the user file. If not an absolute path name, it is treated as being relative to ServerRoot. Each line of the user file contains a user name followed by a colon, followed by the crypt(3) encrypted password.

mod_auth_anon
User Authentication by Anonymous Name/E-Mail Address

■ **Anonymous**   **mod_auth_anon**
Magic User ID for Anonymous Login
Syntax: Anonymous *user* [*user* ...]
Example: Anonymous anonymous ftp http
Default: None
Since: Apache 1.1

This directive specifies one or more *magic* user IDs (*user*) that are allowed access (through HTTP Basic Authentication) without password verification. The user IDs are separated by spaces. You can use quotes or the escape character (a backslash) to insert a space in a *user* argument. Note that the comparison is case-insensitive. The magic user name "anonymous" should always be one of the allowed user IDs.

Use mod_auth_anon's directives to provide a facility similar to Anonymous-FTP.

■ **Anonymous_Authoritative**   **mod_auth_anon**
Fall Through to Other Authorization Methods
Syntax: Anonymous_Authoritative on|off
Example: Anonymous_Authoritative on
Default: Anonymous_Authoritative off
Since: Apache 1.2

When this directive is set to "on", no fall through to other authorization methods occurs. If a user ID does not match any of the values specified in the Anonymous directive, access is denied.

■ **Anonymous_LogEmail**   **mod_auth_anon**
Log the E-Mail Address in the Error Log File
Syntax: Anonymous_LogEmail on|off
Example: Anonymous_LogEmail off
Default: Anonymous_LogEmail on
Since: Apache 1.1

When this directive is set to "on", the default, the entered password (which should contain a sensible e-mail address) is logged in the server error log file.

■ Anonymous_MustGiveEmail   **mod_auth_anon**
Specify Whether Real E-Mail Address Must Be Given as Password
Syntax: `Anonymous_MustGiveEmail on|off`
Example: `Anonymous_MustGiveEmail off`
Default: `Anonymous_MustGiveEmail on`
Since: Apache 1.1

This directive specifies whether the user must give a real e-mail address (*"user@domain"*) as the password on anonymous logins. Blank passwords are then prohibited.

■ Anonymous_NoUserId   **mod_auth_anon**
Specify Whether User IDs Can Be Empty
Syntax: `Anonymous_NoUserId on|off`
Example: `Anonymous_NoUserId on`
Default: `Anonymous_NoUserId off`
Since: Apache 1.1

When this directive is set to "on", users can leave the user ID (and perhaps the password field) empty. This option can prove very convenient for users of GUI-based browsers, who can then simply hit the Return key or click directly on an OK button.

■ Anonymous_VerifyEmail   **mod_auth_anon**
Specify Whether Password Is Checked For Valid E-Mail Address
Syntax: `Anonymous_VerifyEmail on|off`
Example: `Anonymous_VerifyEmail on`
Default: `Anonymous_VerifyEmail off`
Since: Apache 1.1

When this directive is set to "on", the password is checked for at least one "@" and one "." character. It encourages users to enter valid e-mail addresses.

mod_auth_dbm
User Authentication by User Name/Password (UNIX NDBM)

■ AuthDBMAuthoritative   **mod_auth_dbm**
Specify Whether mod_auth_dbm Is the Authority
Syntax: `AuthDBMAuthoritative on|off`
Example: `AuthDBMAuthoritative off`
Default: `AuthDBMAuthoritative on`
Since: Apache 1.2

Setting this directive explicitly to "off" permits for both authentication and authorization to be passed to lower-level modules (as defined in the Configuration and modules.c files) if no user ID or rule matches the supplied user ID. If a user ID or rule is specified, the usual password and access checks are applied and a failure gives an "Authorization Required" reply. Thus, if a user ID appears in the database of more than one module, or if a valid Require directive applies to more than one module, then the first module will verify the credentials and no access will be passed on, regardless of the AuthAuthoritative setting.

AuthDBMGroupFile   mod_auth_dbm

DBM File with Groups for Authentication
Syntax: AuthDBMGroupFile *file*
Example: AuthDBMGroupFile /etc/www-groups.dbm
Default: None
Since: Apache 1.0

This directive specifies the DBM file containing the list of user groups for user authentication. The *file* argument consists of the absolute path to the group file, which is keyed on the user name. The value for a user is a comma-separated list of the groups to which the user belongs. No whitespace can appear within the value, nor any colons. In some cases, it is easier to manage a single database that contains both the password and group details for each user. This approach simplifies any necessary support programs; they must then deal with writing to and locking only a single DBM file. This task can be accomplished by setting the group and password files to point to the same DBM, with the key for the single DBM being the user name. The value then consists of a password section containing the UNIX crypt(3) password, followed by a colon and the comma-separated list of groups. Other data may optionally appear in the DBM file after another colon; the authentication module ignores this information.

Use mod_auth_dbm's or mod_auth_db's directive variants instead of mod_auth's directives if you want to reduce runtime performance penalties.

AuthDBMUserFile   mod_auth_dbm

DBM File with Users for Authentication
Syntax: AuthDBMUserFile *file*
Example: AuthDBMUserFile /etc/www-passwd.dbm
Default: None
Since: Apache 1.0

This directive specifies the DBM file containing the list of users and passwords for user authentication. The *file* argument consists of the absolute path to the user file, which is keyed on the user name. The value for a user is the crypt(3) encrypted password, optionally followed by a colon and arbitrary data. The server ignores the colon and the data following it.

mod_auth_db
User Authentication by User Name/Password (Berkeley-DB)

▣ AuthDBAuthoritative   mod_auth_db
Specify Whether mod_auth_db Is the Authority
Syntax: AuthDBAuthoritative on|off
Example: AuthDBAuthoritative off
Default: AuthDBAuthoritative on
Since: Apache 1.2

Setting this directive explicitly to "off" permits both authentication and authorization to be passed to lower-level modules (as defined in the Configuration and modules.c files) if no user ID or rule matches the supplied user ID. If a user ID or rule is specified, the usual password and access checks are applied and a failure gives an "Authorization Required" reply. If a user ID appears in the database of more than one module, or if a valid Require directive applies to more than one module, then the first module will verify the credentials and no access is allowed, regardless of the AuthAuthoritative setting.

▣ AuthDBGroupFile   mod_auth_db
DB File with Groups for Authentication
Syntax: AuthDBGroupFile *file*
Example: AuthDBGroupFile /etc/www-groups.dbm
Default: None
Since: Apache 1.0

This directive specifies the DB file containing the list of user groups for user authentication. The *file* argument consists of the absolute path to the group file, which is keyed on the user name. The value for a user is a comma-separated list of the groups to which the user belongs. No whitespace can appear within the value, nor any colons.

In some cases, it is easier to manage a single database that contains both the password and group details for each user. This approach simplifies any necessary support programs; they must then deal with writing to and locking only a single DB file. This task can be accomplished by first setting the group and password files to point to the same DB, with the key for the single DB being the username. The value then consists of a password section containing the UNIX crypt(3) password, followed by a colon and the comma-separated list of groups. Other data may optionally appear in the DB file after another colon; the authentication module ignores this information.

■ AuthDBUserFile   mod_auth_db
DB File with Users for Authentication
Syntax: AuthDBUserFile *file*
Example: AuthDBUserFile /etc/www-passwd.dbm
Default: None
Since: Apache 1.0

This directive specifies the DB file containing the list of users and passwords for user authentication. The *file* argument consists of the absolute path to the user file, which is keyed on the user name. The value for a user is the crypt(3) encrypted password, optionally followed by a colon and arbitrary data. The server ignores the colon and the data following it.

mod_digest
User Authentication by User Name/Realm/Password

■ AuthDigestFile   mod_digest
Textual File for Message Digest-based User Authentication
Syntax: AuthDigestFile *filename*
Example: AuthDigestFile etc/passwd.digest
Default: None
Since: Apache 1.1

This directive specifies the textual file containing the list of users and encoded passwords for MD5-based message digest authentication. The *filename* argument consists of the absolute path to the user file. It uses a special format that can be created using the htdigest utility.

4.3.5   Content Selection

mod_dir
Content Selection by Using Directory Default Documents

■ DirectoryIndex   mod_dir
List of Directory Index Files
Syntax: DirectoryIndex *filename* [*filename* ...]
Example: DirectoryIndex index.html welcome.html
Default: DirectoryIndex index.html
Since: Apache 1.0

This directive sets the list of resources for which to search when the client requests an index of a directory by specifying a slash ("/") at the end of the URL. The *filename* is the (%-encoded) URL of a document on the server relative to the requested directory. It usually contains the name of a file in the directory. If several URLs are given, the server will return the first one that it finds. If none of the resources exists and the Indexes option is set, the server will generate its own listing of the directory.

mod_actions
Content Selection by Content Types and Request Methods

■ **Action**   **mod_actions**
Action to Trigger on MIME Type or Internal Handler
Syntax: Action *action-type cgi-script*
Example: Action image/gif /cgi-bin/download
Default: None
Since: Apache 1.1

This directive defines an action that will activate the CGI script *cgi-script* when *action-type* is triggered by a HTTP request. The *action-type* can consist of either an internal handler name or a MIME content type. The URL and file path of the requested document are delivered to *cgi-script* via the standard SSI/CGI PATH_INFO and PATH_TRANSLATED environment variables.

■ **Script**   **mod_actions**
Action to Trigger an HTTP Request Method
Syntax: Script *method cgi-script*
Example: Script PUT /cgi-bin/upload
Default: None
Since: Apache 1.1

This directive defines an action that will activate the CGI script *cgi-script* when a file is requested using the HTTP method of *method* (either GET, POST, PUT, or DELETE). The URL and file path of the requested document are delivered to *cgi-script* via the standard SSI/CGI PATH_IN-FO and PATH_TRANSLATED environment variables. Note that the Script directive defines only *default* actions. If a CGI script, or some other resource that is capable of handling the requested method internally is called, then that action will be taken. Also note that Script will be called with a method of GET only if query arguments are present (such as, "foo.html?bar" for use with HTML ISINDEX-style processing). Otherwise, the request will proceed normally.

mod_negotiation
Content Selection by Best-Matching Client Capabilities

■ CacheNegotiatedDocs   mod_negotiation

Allow Caching of Content-Negotiated Documents
Syntax: `CacheNegotiatedDocs`
Example: `CacheNegotiatedDocs`
Default: `None`
Since: Apache 1.0

This directive allows proxy servers to cache content-negotiated documents. As a result, clients behind those proxies may be able to retrieve versions of the documents that are not the best match for their abilities. This directive applies only to requests that come from HTTP/1.0 browsers. HTTP/1.1 provides much better control over the caching of negotiated documents, and this directive has no effect in responses to HTTP/1.1 requests.

■ LanguagePriority   mod_negotiation

Precedence of Language Variants
Syntax: `LanguagePriority` *lang* [*lang* ...]
Example: `LanguagePriority de en`
Default: `None`
Since: Apache 1.0

This directive sets the precedence of language variants when the client does not express a preference in handling an `Option MultiViews` request. The *lang* arguments appear in order of decreasing preference. For instance, if "LanguagePriority en fr de" is used, then a request for "foo.html", where "foo.html.fr" and "foo.html.de" both exist, but the browser does not express a language preference, will return "foo.html.fr". Note that this directive has an effect only if a "best" language cannot be determined by any other means. Correctly implemented HTTP/1.1 requests will override this directive.

4.3.6   Environment Creation

mod_env
Fixed Environment Variable Creation

- ### PassEnv   **mod_env**
  Pass Environment Variables to SSI/CGI Environment
  Syntax: PassEnv *variable* [*variable* ...]
  Example: PassEnv PATH MANPATH LD_LIBRARY_PATH
  Default: None
  Since: Apache 1.1

  This directive specifies one or more environment variables to pass to SSI/CGI scripts from the server's own process environment.

- ### SetEnv   **mod_env**
  Set an Environment Variable for SSI/CGI Environment
  Syntax: SetEnv *variable value*
  Example: SetEnv PATH /bin:/usr/bin:/usr/local/bin
  Default: None
  Since: Apache 1.1

  This directive sets an environment variable (*variable*) to *value*, which is then passed to SSI/CGI scripts.

- ### UnsetEnv   **mod_env**
  Unset an Environment Variable for SSI/CGI Environment
  Syntax: UnsetEnv *variable* [*variable* ...]
  Example: UnsetEnv LD_LIBRARY_PATH
  Default: None
  Since: Apache 1.1

  This directive removes one or more environment *variable*s from the list of those passed to SSI/CGI scripts.

mod_setenvif
Conditional Environment Variable Creation

- ### BrowserMatch   **mod_setenvif**
  Define Environment Variables Based on User-Agent
  Syntax: BrowserMatch *pattern* [!]*var*[=*val*] [...]
  Example: BrowserMatch "↑Mozilla/[2-4]" ns=24
  Default: None
  Since: Apache 1.2

This directive defines environment variables based on the HTTP `User--Agent` header field. The "BrowserMatch" is equivalent to "SetEnvIf User-Agent" and hence is a deprecated directive name.

■ BrowserMatchNoCase   mod_setenvif
Define Environment Variables Based on HTTP User-Agent (nocase)
Syntax: BrowserMatchNoCase **pattern** [!]*var*[=*val*] [...]
Example: BrowserMatchNoCase "↑Mozilla/[2-4]" ns=24
Default: None
Since: Apache 1.2

This directive defines environment variables based on the HTTP `User--Agent` header field. The "BrowserMatchNoCase" is equivalent to "SetEnvIfNoCase User-Agent" and hence is a deprecated directive name.

■ SetEnvIf   mod_setenvif
Define Environment Variables Based on HTTP Attributes
Syntax: SetEnvIf **attribute** **pattern** [!]*var*[=*val*] [...]
Example: SetEnvIf Request_URI ".*\.gif$" isgif
Default: None
Since: Apache 1.3

This directive defines environment variables based on attributes of the HTTP request. The **attribute** arguments can take on the values of various HTTP request header fields (see RFC 2068 for more information) or other aspects of the request. For example, the following values are valid: "Remote_Host" for the host name (if available) of the client making the request; "Remote_Addr" for the IP address of the client making the request; "Remote_User" for the authenticated user name (if available); "Request_Method" for the name of the method being used (such as GET or POST); "Request_Protocol" for the name and version of the protocol with which the request was made (such as "HTTP/0.9" or "HTTP/1.1") or "Request_URI" for the portion of the URL following the scheme and host portion.

Use SetEnvIf in conjunction with CustomLog to provide conditionalized logging — for instance to not writing the log entries for requests of inline images.

Some of the more commonly used request header field names include "Host", "User-Agent", and "Referer". If the **attribute** doesn't match any of the special keywords or any of the request's header field names, it is tested to see whether it matches the name of an environment variable in the list of those associated with the request. SetEnvIf directives can therefore test it against the result of prior matches. Only those environment variables defined by earlier SetEnvIf or SetEnvIfNoCase directives are available for testing in this manner; that is, these variables must have been defined at a broader scope (such as server-wide) or previously in the current directive's scope.

■ **SetEnvIfNoCase**   **mod_setenvif**
Define Environment Variables Based on HTTP Attributes (nocase)
Syntax: SetEnvIfNoCase *attribute pattern* [!]*var*[=*val*]
Example: SetEnvIfNoCase Request_URI "\.ps$" isps
Default: None
Since: Apache 1.3

This directive is semantically identical to the SetEnvIf directive. It
differs only in that the regular expression matching is performed in a
case-insensitive manner.

mod_unique_id
Generation of Unique Identifiers by Request

This module provides no directives!

4.3.7   Server-Side Scripting

mod_cgi
Common Gateway Interface (CGI) Implementation

■ **ScriptLog**   **mod_cgi**
Error Log File for CGI Scripts
Syntax: ScriptLog *filename*
Example: ScriptLog logs/script_log
Default: None
Since: Apache 1.2

ScriptLog allows you
to debug your CGI
scripts by writing
debug information to
stderr.

This directive sets the error log file for CGI scripts. Without this directive, no error logging is done. With it, any output to stderr of the
CGI scripts is logged into *filename*. If this argument is a relative path
name, it is taken as being relative to ServerRoot. The log file will be
opened as the user run as the CGI child processes — that is, the user
specified in the main User directive. Consequently, either the directory containing the *filename* must be writable by that user or the file
must be manually created and set to be writable by that user. Note that
script logging is meant to serve as a debugging feature when you are
writing CGI scripts; it should not be activated continuously on running
servers.

▣ ScriptLogBuffer   **mod_cgi**
Size of Logged Data from PUT and POST Requests
Syntax: ScriptLogBuffer *bytes*
Example: ScriptLogBuffer 2048
Default: ScriptLogBuffer 1024
Since: Apache 1.2

This directive limits the size of the PUT and POST request bodies that are logged to the ScriptLog file. It prevents the log file from growing too quickly if large request bodies are received.

▣ ScriptLogLength   **mod_cgi**
Maximum Size of CGI Error Log File
Syntax: ScriptLogLength *bytes*
Example: ScriptLogLength 512000
Default: ScriptLogLength 10385760
Since: Apache 1.2

This directive limits the size of the CGI script log file. Because this file holds a great deal of information for each CGI error (all request headers, all script output), it can grow quite large. To prevent problems caused by unbounded growth, you can use this directive to set a maximum file size (in bytes) for the CGI log file. If the file exceeds this size, no more information will be written to it.

mod_include
Server-Side Includes (SSI) Implementation

▣ XBitHack   **mod_include**
Treat Ordinary HTML Documents as SSI Documents
Syntax: XBitHack *mode*
Example: XBitHack full
Default: XBitHack off
Since: Apache 1.0

This directive controls the parsing of ordinary HTML documents if the execution bit is set on them. It affects only files associated with the MIME type text/html. The *mode* argument can have the following values: "off" for no special treatment of executable files; "on" for treatment of any file that has the user-execute bit set as a server-parsed HTML document (SSI); or "full" for the same as "on", plus testing of the group-execute bit. If the latter bit is set, then the HTTP "Last-Modified" date of the returned file is set to be the last modified

Use "XBitHack on" if you want to turn some plain HTML pages into HTML pages with SSI directives without having to change your URLs.

time of the file. If the group-execute bit is not set, then no "Last-Modified" date is set. Setting this bit allows clients and proxies to cache the result of the request.

4.3.8   Response Header Generation

mod_mime
Fixed Content Type/Encoding Assignment

■ **AddEncoding**   **mod_mime**
Associate MIME Content Encoding with File Extension
Syntax: AddEncoding *mime-enc file-ext* [*file-ext* . . .]
Example: AddEncoding x-gzip .gz
Default: None
Since: Apache 1.0

This directive maps a given file name extension to the specified MIME encoding type one or more times. The *mime-enc* argument is the MIME encoding used for documents with the file extension *file-ext*. This mapping is added to any already in force, and it overrides any existing mappings for the same extension.

■ **AddHandler**   **mod_mime**
Associate Content Handler with File Extension
Syntax: AddHandler *handler file-ext* [*file-ext* . . .]
Example: AddHandler cgi-script .cgi
Default: None
Since: Apache 1.1

This directive maps a given file name extension *file-ext* to the handler *handler* one or more times. This mapping is added to any already in force, and it overrides any existing mappings for the same extension.

■ **AddLanguage**   **mod_mime**
Associate MIME Content Language with File Extension
Syntax: AddLanguage *mime-lang file-ext* [*file-ext* . . .]
Example: AddLanguage de .de
Default: None
Since: Apache 1.0

This directive maps a given file name extension *file-ext* to the specified MIME content language *mime-lang* one or more times. The mime-lang argument is the MIME language of documents with the specified extension. This mapping is added to any already in force, and it overrides any existing mappings for the same extension.

■ **AddType**   **mod_mime**

Associate MIME Content Type with File Extension
Syntax: AddType *mime-type file-ext* [*file-ext* ...]
Example: AddType image/gif .gif
Default: None
Since: Apache 1.0

This directive maps a given file name extension *file-ext* to the specified MIME content type one or more times. The *mime-type* argument is the MIME type to use for file names with the *file-ext* file extension. This mapping is added to any already in force, and it overrides any existing mappings for the same extension. This directive can be used to add mappings not listed in the MIME types file (see the TypesConfig directive below).

■ **DefaultLanguage**   **mod_mime**

Define Default MIME Content Language
Syntax: DefaultLanguage *mime-lang*
Example: DefaultLanguage en
Default: None
Since: Apache 1.1

This directive tells Apache that all files in the directive's scope (for example, all files covered by the current <Directory> container) that don't have an explicit language extension (such as ".de" or ".en" as configured by AddLanguage) should be considered to be in the specified *mime-lang* language. Consequently, entire directories can be marked as containing content of a particular language, without having to rename each file. Unlike with the use of extensions to specify languages, DefaultLanguage can specify only a single language. If no Default-Language directive is in force, and a file does not have any language extensions as configured by AddLanguage, then that file will be considered to have no language attribute.

■ **ForceType**   **mod_mime**

Force a Default MIME Content Type
Syntax: ForceType *mime-type*
Example: ForceType application/octet-stream
Default: None
Since: Apache 1.1

When placed into an .htaccess file or a <Directory> or <Location> section, this directive forces all matching files to be served as the MIME content type given by *mime-type*. Note that it overrides any file name extensions that might determine the media type.

■ **RemoveHandler**   **mod_mime**
Remove a Content Handler Association
Syntax: RemoveHandler *file-ext* [*file-ext* ...]
Example: RemoveHandler .html .cgi
Default: None
Since: Apache 1.1

This directive removes any handler associations for files with the given extensions. Consequently, .htaccess files in subdirectories can undo any associations inherited from parent directories or the server configuration files.

■ **SetHandler**   **mod_mime**
Add a Content Handler Association
Syntax: SetHandler *handler-name*
Example: SetHandler server-status
Default: None
Since: Apache 1.1

When placed into an .htaccess file or a <Directory> or <Location> section, this directive forces all matching files to be parsed through the handler given by *handler-name*.

■ **TypesConfig**   **mod_mime**
Configuration for Mapping File Extensions to MIME Content Types
Syntax: TypesConfig *filename*
Example: TypesConfig /etc/httpd/mime.types
Default: TypesConfig conf/mime.types
Since: Apache 1.0

This directive sets the location of the configuration file that maps file extensions to MIME content types. Alternatively, you can use the Add-Type directive for the same purpose. The *filename* argument is relative to the ServerRoot. It contains lines in the same format as the arguments to an AddType command: *"MIME-type extension extension ..."*. The extensions are lowercase, and blank lines and lines beginning with a hash character ("#") are ignored.

mod_mime_magic
Automatic Content Type/Encoding Assignment

▦ **MimeMagicFile**   **mod_mime_magic**
File with MIME Type Magic Matchings
Syntax: MimeMagicFile *file*
Example: MimeMagicFile conf/mime.magic
Default: None
Since: Apache 1.3

This directive can be used to enable the mod_mime_magic module. Thus, if mod_mime could not find a MIME content type for a document, the mod_mime_magic module can use *file* to guess the content type of the requested document from its first bytes.

mod_mime_magic is for Apache what file(1) is for UNIX.

mod_expires
Creation of HTTP Expires Header

▦ **ExpiresActive**   **mod_expires**
Trigger Expires Header Generation
Syntax: ExpiresActive on|off
Example: ExpiresActive on
Default: ExpiresActive off
Since: Apache 1.2

This directive enables or disables the generation of the Expires header. If found in an .htaccess file, for instance, it applies only to documents generated from that directory. If the directive is set to "on", the Expires header will be added to served documents according to the criteria defined by the ExpiresByType and ExpiresDefault directives. Note that this directive does not guarantee the generation of an Expires header. If the criteria are not met, no header will be sent, just as if this directive had not been specified.

▦ **ExpiresByType**   **mod_expires**
Generate Expires Header for a Particular Document MIME Type
Syntax: ExpiresByType *MIME-type codeseconds*
Example: ExpiresByType image/gif A2592000
Default: None
Since: Apache 1.2

This directive defines the value of the Expires header generated for documents of the specified MIME type. The *second* argument specifies the number of seconds that will be added to a base time to construct the

Use ExpiresByType to control the individual caching for your files.

expiration date. This base time is either the time when the file was last modified or the time when the client accessed the document. It is specified by the *code* field, where "M" means that the file's last modification time should be used as the base time, and "A" means the client's access time should be used. The difference in effect is subtle. If "M" is used, all current copies of the document in all caches will expire at the same time, which can be good for a weekly notice that's always found at the same URL, for example. If "A" is used, the date of expiration differs for each client; this choice can be effective for image files that don't change very often, for example, and particularly for a set of related documents that all refer to the same images.

■ ExpiresDefault   mod_expires
Default Value for Generation of Expires Header
Syntax: ExpiresDefault *codeseconds*
Example: ExpiresDefault M86400
Default: None
Since: Apache 1.2

This directive sets the default for calculating the expiration time for all documents in the affected realm. It can be overridden on a type-by-type basis by the ExpiresByType directive. The syntax of the *code-seconds* argument is the same as that for ExpiresByType.

mod_headers
Creation of Arbitrary HTTP Headers

■ Header   mod_headers
Control HTTP Response Header Fields
Syntax: Header *operation header* [*value*]
Example: Header set Author "John Doe"
Default: None
Since: Apache 1.2

Use Header for creating customized HTTP response header fields.

This directive can replace, merge, or remove HTTP response headers fields. It performs the *operation* designated by the first argument. This argument can have any of four values. The "set" value sets the response *header* to *value*, replacing any previous header with this name. The "append" value appends *value* to the response *header* of the same name; when a new value is merged into an existing header, it is separated from the existing header with a comma — the HTTP standard way of giving a header multiple values. The "add" value adds *value* to the response *header* in the existing set of headers, even if this header already exists. The addition can result in two (or more) headers having the same name (and lead to unforeseen consequences; in general, "append" should be used instead). The "unset" value removes the response *header*, if it exists. If multiple headers of the same name exist, all will be removed.

The *operation* argument is followed by a *header* name, which can include the final colon, though it is not required. Case is ignored. For "add", "append", and "set" operations, a *value* is given as the third argument. If this value contains spaces, it should be surrounded by double quotes. For "unset", no value should be given.

mod_cern_meta
Creation of Arbitrary HTTP Headers (CERN-style)

■ **MetaFiles**   **mod_cern_meta**
Trigger CERN Meta-file Processing
Syntax: MetaFiles on|off
Example: MetaFiles on
Default: MetaFiles off
Since: Apache 1.3

This directive enables or disables meta-file processing on a per-directory basis. Meta-files were a feature of the CERN httpd, and this functionality exists to provide backward compatibility.

■ **MetaDir**   **mod_cern_meta**
Subdirectory Containing CERN Meta-files
Syntax: MetaDir *subdir*
Example: MetaDir .meta
Default: MetaDir .web
Since: Apache 1.1

This directive specifies the name of the subdirectory *subdir* holding CERN-style meta-files. The subdirectory is usually "hidden" within the directory that contains the file being accessed. Set *subdir* to "." to let Apache look in the same directory holding the accessed file.

■ **MetaSuffix**   **mod_cern_meta**
File Name Suffix of CERN Meta-files
Syntax: MetaSuffix *suffix*
Example: MetaSuffix .meta
Default: MetaSuffix .meta
Since: Apache 1.1

This directive specifies the file name *suffix* for the file containing the CERN meta-information. For example, the default values for the Meta-Dir and MetaSuffix directives will send a request to "*DocumentRoot*/somedir/index.html" to look in "*DocumentRoot*/somedir/.web/index.html.meta" and will use its contents to generate additional MIME response header information.

4.3.9   Internal Content Handlers

mod_asis
Generation of Raw Responses

This module provides no directives!

mod_autoindex
Generation of Directory Index Documents

■ **AddAlt**   **mod_autoindex**
Alternative Text for File Icon
Syntax: AddAlt *text file* [*file* ...]
Example: AddAlt "TGZ" *.tar.gz
Default: None
Since: Apache 1.0

This directive sets (one or more times) the alternative *text* to display for a *file* — instead of an icon, for FancyIndexing. The *file* argument can contain a file extension, partial file name, wildcard expression, or full file name. The *text* argument consists of a string enclosed in double quotes. This alternative text is displayed if the client cannot show the image or has image loading disabled.

■ **AddAltByEncoding**   **mod_autoindex**
Alternative Text for File Icon (by MIME Encoding)
Syntax: AddAltByEncoding *text enc* [*enc* ...]
Example: AddAltByEncoding "GZIP" x-gzip
Default: None
Since: Apache 1.0

This directive sets (one or more times) the alternative *text* to display for a file with the MIME encoding *enc*, instead of an icon, for FancyIndexing. The *mime-enc* argument must be a valid MIME content encoding. The *text* argument is enclosed in double quotes. This alternative text is displayed if the client cannot show the image or has image loading disabled.

■ **AddAltByType** **mod_autoindex**

Alternate Text for File Icon (by MIME Type)

Syntax: AddAltByType *text mime-type* [*mime-type* ...]

Example: AddAltByType "HTML" text/html

Default: None

Since: Apache 1.0

This directive sets (one or more times) the alternative *text* to display for a file with the MIME type *mime-type*, instead of an icon, for FancyIndexing. The *mime-type* argument must be a valid MIME content type. The *text* argument is enclosed in double quotes. This alternative text is displayed if the client cannot show the image or has image loading disabled.

■ **AddDescription** **mod_autoindex**

Description Text for File

Syntax: AddDescription *text file* [*file* ...]

Example: AddDescription "Obsolete" foo-*.tar.gz

Default: None

Since: Apache 1.0

This directive sets (one or more times) the description *text* to display for a *file* for FancyIndexing. The *file* argument can contain a file extension, partial file name, wildcard expression, or full file name. The *text* argument is enclosed in double quotes and can be a maximum of 23 characters long. Seven more characters may be added if the directory is covered by an "IndexOptions SuppressSize", and 19 characters may be added if "IndexOptions SuppressLastModified" is in effect. The absolute maximum width of this column is therefore 49 characters.

Use AddDescription to annotate the automatically generated directory listings.

■ **AddIcon** **mod_autoindex**

Image for File Icon

Syntax: AddIcon *icon file* [*file* ...]

Example: AddIcon (IMG,/foo.xbm) .gif .jpg

Default: None

Since: Apache 1.0

This directive sets (one or more times) the icon to display next to a *file* for FancyIndexing. The *icon* argument either contains a %-escaped relative URL to the icon or has the format "(*alttext*,*url*)" where *alttext* is the text tag given for an icon for non-graphical browsers. The *file* argument can be either "↑↑DIRECTORY↑↑" for directories, "↑↑BLANKICON↑↑" for blank lines (to format the list correctly), a file extension, a wildcard expression, a partial file name, or a complete file name.

■ AddIconByEncoding   **mod_autoindex**
Image for File Icon (by MIME Encoding)
Syntax: `AddIconByEncoding` *icon enc* [*enc ...*]
Example: `AddIconByEncoding (IMG,/foo.xbm) x-zip`
Default: `None`
Since: Apache 1.0

This directive is similar to `AddIcon`, except that a MIME encoding is used for matching purposes instead of a file. The *enc* argument is a wildcard expression matching the required content encoding.

■ AddIconByType   **mod_autoindex**
Image for File Icon (by MIME Type)
Syntax: `AddIconByType` *icon type* [*type ...*]
Example: `AddIconByType (IMG,/foo.xbm) image/*`
Default: `None`
Since: Apache 1.0

This directive is similar to `AddIcon`, except that a MIME content type is used for matching purposes instead of a file. The *type* argument is a wildcard expression matching the required content type.

■ DefaultIcon   **mod_autoindex**
Default Icon Image
Syntax: `DefaultIcon` *url*
Example: `DefaultIcon /icon/unknown.xbm`
Default: `None`
Since: Apache 1.0

This directive sets the icon to display for files when no specific icon is known, for `FancyIndexing`. The *url* argument consists a %-escaped relative URL to the icon image.

■ FancyIndexing   **mod_autoindex**
Enable or Disable Fancy Directory Indexing (Deprecated)
Syntax: `FancyIndexing on|off`
Example: `FancyIndexing on`
Default: `FancyIndexing off`
Since: Apache 1.0

This directive sets the `FancyIndexing` option for a directory. It has been deprecated, however, and the `IndexOptions` directive should be used instead.

▪ HeaderName   mod_autoindex
Document to Be Inserted at the Top of Index Listings
Syntax: HeaderName *filename*
Example: HeaderName /common/header.html
Default: None
Since: Apache 1.0

This directive sets the name of the document that will be inserted at the top of an index listing. The *filename* argument contains the name of the file to include and is treated as a URI path relative to the one used to access the directory being indexed. It must resolve to a document with a major content type of "text" (for example, "text/html" or "text/plain").

▪ IndexIgnore   mod_autoindex
Files to Ignore in Index Listings
Syntax: IndexIgnore *file* [*file* ...]
Example: IndexIgnore .htaccess *.bak *~
Default: None
Since: Apache 1.0

This directive adds to the list of files that should be ignored when listing a directory. Each *file* argument is a file extension, partial file name, wildcard expression, or full file name. Multiple IndexIgnore directives add to the list of ignored files, rather than replacing them. By default, the list contains "." to ignore all UNIX "dot-files."

▪ IndexOptions   mod_autoindex
Enable or Disable Particular Indexing Options
Syntax: IndexOptions [+|-]*option* [[+|-]*option* ...]
Example: IndexOptions FancyIndexing IconsAreLinks
Default: None
Since: Apache 1.0

This directive specifies the behavior of the directory indexing. The *option* arguments can have any of the following values. "FancyIndexing" for turns on fancy indexing of directories; "IconHeight[=*pixels*]" to cause the server to include HEIGHT and WIDTH HTML attributes in the IMG tag for the file icon. "IconsAreLinks" makes the icons part of the anchor for the file name (for fancy indexing); "IconWidth[=*pixels*]" causes the server to include HTML HEIGHT and WIDTH attributes in the IMG tag for the file icon. "NameWidth=[*n*—*]" specifies the width of the file name column in characters (if the keyword value is "*", the column is automatically sized to the length of the longest file name in the display). "ScanHTMLTitles" enables the extraction of the title from

HTML documents for fancy indexing. "SuppressColumnSorting" ensures that the column headings in a fancy indexed directory listing are not turned into links for sorting. "SuppressDescription" suppresses the file description in fancy indexing listings. "SuppressHTML-Preamble" assumes that the HeaderName document also provides the standard HTML preamble (HTML, HEAD, and other tags). "Suppress-LastModified" suppresses the display of the last modification date in fancy indexing listings. "SuppressSize" suppresses the file size in fancy indexing listings.

■ IndexOrderDefault   mod_autoindex

Order of Documents in Index Listings
Syntax: IndexIgnore *type keyword*
Example: IndexIgnore Ascending Name
Default: None
Since: Apache 1.0

This directive is used in combination with the FancyIndexing index option. By default, fancy indexed directory listings are displayed in ascending order by file name. The IndexOrderDefault directive allows you to change this initial display order. It takes two arguments. The first argument, *type*, must be either "Ascending" or "Descending", indicating the direction of the sort. The second argument, *keyword*, must be one of the keywords "Name", "Date", "Size", or "Description" and identifies the primary key. The secondary key is always the ascending file name.

■ ReadmeName   mod_autoindex

Document Appended to Index Listings
Syntax: ReadmeName *filename*
Example: ReadmeName README.txt
Default: None
Since: Apache 1.0

This directive sets the name of the document that will be appended to the end of the index listing. The *filename* argument (the name of the file to include) is treated as a URI path relative to the one used to access the directory being indexed. It must resolve to a document with a major content type of "text" (for example, "text/html" or "text/plain").

mod_status
Display Summary of Server Runtime Information

■ **ExtendedStatus**   **mod_status**

Enable Extended Server Status Information
Syntax: `ExtendedStatus on|off`
Example: `ExtendedStatus on`
Default: `ExtendedStatus off`
Since: Apache 1.3

This directive can be used to show extended status information in the server status pages displayed by `mod_status`. It also controls whether the server keeps track of extended status information for each request. This setting applies to the entire server; that is, it cannot be enabled or disabled on a virtual-host-by-virtual-host basis.

mod_info
Display Summary of Server Configuration-Time Information

■ **AddModuleInfo**   **mod_info**

Add Extra Information to Description of a Module
Syntax: `AddModuleInfo` *module-source string*
Example: `AddModuleInfo mod_ssl.c "SSL/TLS"`
Default: `None`
Since: Apache 1.3

This directive allows the content of *string* to be shown as additional information for the module *module-source* in `mod_info`'s generated web pages.

4.3.10   Request Logging

mod_log_config
Generic Request Logging

■ **CookieLog**   **mod_log_config**

Log File for HTTP Cookies
Syntax: `CookieLog` *file*
Example: `CookieLog logs/cookie.log`
Default: `None`
Since: Apache 1.0

This directive sets the *file* for logging of HTTP cookies. The *file* argument is relative to the ServerRoot. This directive is included only for compatibility purposes and has been deprecated.

■ **CustomLog**   **mod_log_config**
Customized Log File Facility
Syntax: CustomLog *file format* [env=[!]*variable*]
Example: CustomLog logs/access "%h \"%r\" %s %b"
Default: None
Since: Apache 1.2

The CustomLog directive allows you to create arbitrary access log files. In conjunction with SetEnvIf you even can conditionalize them.

This directive enables you to write a customized log file, where each log file line is formatted according to the specification given in *format*. If the "env=.." construct is appended, the writing of a line can be conditionalized through the existence or nonexistence of an environment variable (usually created by mod_setenvif or mod_rewrite based on the particular HTTP request). The options for the format match those available for the argument of the LogFormat directive. If the *format* argument includes any spaces (as it will in almost all cases), it should be enclosed in double quotes. Instead of an actual format string, you can also use a format nickname defined with the LogFormat directive.

■ **LogFormat**   **mod_log_config**
Define a Customized Log File Format
Syntax: LogFormat *format* [*nickname*]
Example: LogFormat "%h %l %u %t \"%r\" %s %b" clf
Default: None
Since: Apache 1.0

Use LogFormat to pre-configure log formats if you need them in lots of <VirtualHost> sections.

This directive sets the *format* of the default log file set by the TransferLog directive or defines a customized format that is available under *nickname* to the CustomLog directive.

■ **TransferLog**   **mod_log_config**
Default Transfer and Access Log File
Syntax: TransferLog *file*
Example: TransferLog logs/access.log
Default: None
Since: Apache 1.0

This directive defines a log file in the format specified by the most recent LogFormat directive, or in the *Common Log Format* (CLF) if no other default format has been specified. The *file* argument is either (1) a file name relative to ServerRoot or (2) "|" followed by a shell command to receive the log file information via stdin.

mod_log_agent
Specialized User-Agent Logging (Deprecated)

■ AgentLog   mod_log_agent
Log File for HTTP User-Agent Header Fields (Deprecated)
Syntax: AgentLog *file*
Example: AgentLog logs/agent.log
Default: None
Since: Apache 1.0

This directive specifies the *file* to which the server will log the HTTP
User-Agent header field of incoming requests. It has been deprecated,
however, and you should use the CustomLog directive with the format
string "%{User-Agent}i" instead.

mod_log_referer
Specialized Referrer Logging (Deprecated)

■ RefererIgnore   mod_log_referer
Exclude HTTP Referer Header Fields from Logging (Deprecated)
Syntax: RefererIgnore *string* [*string* ...]
Example: RefererIgnore www.foo.dom
Default: None
Since: Apache 1.0

This directive adds to the list of strings that should be ignored in HTTP
Referer header fields. If any of the *string* arguments in the list is contained in the Referer header field, then no referrer information will be
logged for the request.

■ RefererLog   mod_log_referer
Log File for HTTP Referer Header Fields (Deprecated)
Syntax: RefererLog *file*
Example: RefererLog logs/referer.log
Default: None
Since: Apache 1.0

This directive specifies the *file* to which the server will log the HTTP
Referer header field of incoming requests. It has been deprecated,
however, and you should use the CustomLog directive with the format
string "%{Referer}i" instead.

mod_usertrack
Specialized User Click-Trail Logging

■ **CookieExpires**   **mod_usertrack**

Expiry Time of Tracking Cookies
Syntax: CookieExpires *expiry-time*
Example: CookieExpires "2 days"
Default: None
Since: Apache 1.2

This directive sets an expiry time on the HTTP cookie generated by mod_usertrack. The expiry period can be given either as a number of seconds or in a format such as "2 weeks 3 days 7 hours". Valid denominations are "years", "months", "weeks", "hours", "minutes", and "seconds". If *expiry-time* appears in any format other than one number indicating the number of seconds, enclose it in double quotes. If this directive is not used, HTTP cookies persist only for the duration of the current browser session.

■ **CookieName**   **mod_usertrack**

Name of Tracking Cookie
Syntax: CookieName *name*
Example: CookieName FooBar
Default: CookieName Apache
Since: Apache 1.3.7

This directive specifies the HTTP cookie that mod_usertrack uses for tracking purposes. By default, this cookie is named "Apache". You must specify a valid cookie name. Using a name containing unusual characters will yield unpredictable results. A valid name is one that matches the regular expression "[A-Za-z0-9_-]+".

Do not use
"CookieTracking on"
in practice — the whole
mechanism is only
theoretically usable.

■ **CookieTracking**   **mod_usertrack**

Cookie Tracking Operation Switch
Syntax: CookieTracking on|off
Example: CookieTracking on
Default: CookieTracking off
Since: Apache 1.2

When mod_usertrack is compiled into Apache and "CookieTracking on" is set, Apache will start sending a user-tracking HTTP cookie for all new requests. This directive can be used to turn this behavior on or off on a per-server or per-directory basis. By default, cookie tracking is not activated.

4.3.11 Experimental

mod_mmap_static
Caching of Frequently Served Pages via Memory Mapping

■ **MMapFile**   **mod_mmap_static**
Memory-Map a Document for Faster Delivery
Syntax: MMapFile *file* [*file* ...]
Example: MMapFile /www/index.html
Default: None
Since: Apache 1.3

This directive maps one or more files (given as whitespace-separated arguments in *file*) into memory at server start-up to speed up the document's delivery. The files are automatically unmapped upon server shutdown. When the files have changed on the file system, you must send at least a SIGHUP or SIGUSR1 signal to the server to remap them. Use this experimental functionality with care, however. Keep in mind that the document content is not re-mapped automatically by mod_mmap_static — hence the "static" in the module's name.

MMapFile is experimental and has restrictions, so use it with care!

mod_example
Apache API Demonstration (Developers Only)

■ **Example**   **mod_example**
Example Module Operation Switch
Syntax: Example
Example: Example
Default: None
Since: Apache 1.2

This pure example directive, which is implemented by mod_example, is mainly intended for use by developers who want to understand the Apache API. Do not use it on production servers. It simply raises a flag when the example content handler executes for a request (usually activated via "SetHandler example-handler" in a <Location> or <File> container for a particular location or file type). If you browse to a URL to which this example content handler applies, you will see a display of the routines within the module and learn how and in what order they were called to service the document request.

The mod_example is for developers only!

4.3.12   Extensional Functionality

mod_proxy
Caching Proxy Implementation for HTTP and FTP

■ **ProxyRequests**   **mod_proxy**
Proxy Module Operation Switch
Syntax: ProxyRequests on|off
Example: ProxyRequests on
Default: ProxyRequests off
Since: Apache 1.1

Keep in mind that
mod_proxy is only
HTTP/1.0 compliant
and still not HTTP/1.1.

This directive allows or prevents Apache from functioning as an HTTP
proxy server (in addition to its usual behavior as an HTTP origin server).
Setting this directive to "off" does not disable mod_proxy, however.
For instance, proxy requests internally generated by ProxyPass or RewriteRule directives continue to be processed.

■ **AllowCONNECT**   **mod_proxy**
Ports to Which the HTTP CONNECT Method Is Allowed to Connect
Syntax: AllowCONNECT port [port ...]
Example: AllowCONNECT 443 563 8443 8563
Default: None
Since: Apache 1.3

This directive configures the ports to which the HTTP CONNECT proxy
method is allowed to connect. By default, only the HTTPS (443) and
SNEWS (563) ports are allowed.

■ **NoProxy**   **mod_proxy**
Targets to Which the Proxy Will Connect Directly
Syntax: NoProxy target [target ...]
Example: NoProxy .foo.dom 192.168.1.0/21
Default: None
Since: Apache 1.3

This directive specifies a space-separated list of *target*s — that is, sub-
nets ("192.168.1.0/21"), IP addresses ("192.168.1.1"), hosts ("www.-
foo.dom"), and domains (".foo.dom") — to which the proxy will connect directly, without using a ProxyRemote — specified forwarding
proxy. This directive is mainly useful for Apache proxy servers that
reside within intranets.

■ **ProxyRemote**   **mod_proxy**
Forward Proxy Requests to Other Proxies
Syntax: ProxyRemote *url-pattern remote-proxy*
Example: ProxyRemote * http://remote-server:3128
Default: None
Since: Apache 1.1

This directive defines remote proxy servers for use by the local proxy
server. The *url-pattern* can be the name of a URL scheme that the remote server supports, a partial URL for which the remote server should
be used, or "*" to indicate that the server should be contacted for all requests. The *remote-proxy* is a partial URL for the remote proxy server.

Configure top-level
proxy servers with
ProxyRemote.

■ **ProxyBlock**   **mod_proxy**
Block Proxy Connections to Targets
Syntax: ProxyBlock *target* [*target* ...]
Example: ProxyBlock cybersex *.sex.com
Default: None
Since: Apache 1.2

This directive specifies a list of URL substrings, host names, and domain names, separated by spaces. The proxy server will block HTTP,
HTTPS, and FTP document requests to those targets. In addition, mod_-
proxy will attempt to determine the IP addresses of those list items that
may be host names during start-up and use them for matching. The
special target "*" blocks all proxy connections.

■ **ProxyDomain**   **mod_proxy**
Default Intranet Domain Name
Syntax: ProxyDomain *domain-name*
Example: ProxyDomain .mycompany.com
Default: None
Since: Apache 1.3

This directive is useful only for Apache proxy servers that reside within
intranets. It specifies the default domain name (*domain-name*) to which
the Apache proxy server will belong. If a proxy request to a host without a domain name is encountered, the directive will generate a redirection response to the same host with the configured *domain-name*
appended.

◼ ProxyReceiveBufferSize   **mod_proxy**
Explicit Network Buffer Size for Outgoing Proxy Connections
Syntax: `ProxyReceiveBufferSize` *bytes*
Example: `ProxyReceiveBufferSize 2048`
Default: `None`
Since: Apache 1.3

This directive specifies an explicit network buffer size for outgoing HTTP, HTTPS, and FTP connections, so as to increase throughput. The buffer size must be greater than 512 or set to 0 to indicate that the operating system's default buffer size should be used.

◼ ProxyVia   **mod_proxy**
Control the Use of the HTTP Via Header Field for the Proxy
Syntax: `ProxyVia off|on|full|block`
Example: `ProxyVia full`
Default: `ProxyVia off`
Since: Apache 1.3

This directive controls the use of the HTTP `Via` header field by the proxy server, thereby managing the flow of proxy requests along a chain of proxy servers. See RFC 2068 (HTTP/1.1) for an explanation of `Via` header fields. If set to "`off`" (the default), no special processing is performed. If a request or reply then contains a `Via` header field, it passes through unchanged. If set to "`on`", however, a `Via` header field will be added to each request and response for the current proxy server. If set to "`full`", each generated `Via` header field will have the Apache server version shown as a `Via` comment field. If set to "`block`", every proxy request will have all its `Via` header fields removed and no new `Via` header field will be generated.

◼ ProxyPass   **mod_proxy**
Map Remote Servers into Local URL Space
Syntax: `ProxyPass` *local-path remote-url*
Example: `ProxyPass /foo/ http://www.foo.dom/`
Default: `None`
Since: Apache 1.1

Use ProxyPass to virtually map areas of remote web servers into your own web space.

This directive allows remote servers to be mapped into the URL space of the local server. In this situation, the local server does not act as an HTTP proxy in the conventional sense, but optically appears to mirror the remote server. The *local-path* argument is the name of a local virtual path, and the *remote-url* argument is a partial URL for the remote server. Requests under *local-path* on the local server will be translated into requests under *remote-url* in the background. More flexi-

ble mapping can be achieved by using the proxy flag of mod_rewrite's
RewriteRule directive.

■ ProxyPassReverse   **mod_proxy**
Adjust HTTP Redirect Responses
Syntax: ProxyPassReverse *local-path remote-url*
Example: ProxyPassReverse /ab/ http://www.ab.dom/
Default: None
Since: Apache 1.3

This mod_proxy directive adjusts the URL in the Location header field
on HTTP redirect responses sent by remote hosts. This adjustment is
essential, for instance, when Apache is used as a "reverse proxy." In
this case, it avoids by-passing the reverse proxy because HTTP redirects on the back-end servers that stay behind the reverse proxy. The
local-path argument is the name of a local virtual path, and the *remote-
url* argument is a partial URL for the remote server — just as with
the ProxyPass directive. Usually, the directive is used in conjunction
with ProxyPass, but ProxyPassReverse can also be used in conjunction with the proxy flag of mod_rewrite's RewriteRule directive.

ProxyPassReverse is
important for "remote
proxy" situations — for
instance in a load
balancing environment.

■ NoCache   **mod_proxy**
Targets for Which the Proxy Will Not Perform Caching
Syntax: NoCache *target* [*target* ...]
Example: NoCache .foo.dom 192.168.1.0/21
Default: None
Since: Apache 1.1

This directive specifies a space-seperated list of *target*s — that is, sub-
nets ("192.168.1.0/21"), IP addresses ("192.168.1.1"), hosts ("www.-
foo.dom"), and domains (".foo.dom") — for which the proxy will not
cache documents. This directive is mainly useful for Apache proxy
servers that reside within intranets.

■ CacheRoot   **mod_proxy**
Filesystem Root of the Proxy Document Cache
Syntax: CacheRoot *directory*
Example: CacheRoot /usr/local/apache/var/cache
Default: None
Since: Apache 1.1

This directive configures *directory* to be the location where the proxy
stores cached documents. Using this directive implicitly enables caching. If no CacheRoot is defined, proxy functionality will be available if
ProxyRequests are set to "on", but no caching will be available.

■ CacheSize   **mod_proxy**
Maximum Disk Space Used for the Proxy Document Cache
Syntax: CacheSize *size*
Example: CacheSize 1024
Default: None
Since: Apache 1.1

This directive sets the maximum disk space used by the document cache in kilobytes. Although usage may exceed this setting, the garbage collection will subsequently delete files until the usage is at or lower than this size. Depending on the expected proxy traffic volume and CacheGcInterval, use a value that is at least 20% to 40% lower than the available disk space.

■ CacheDirLength   **mod_proxy**
Subdirectory Name Length for the Proxy Document Cache
Syntax: CacheDirLength *length*
Example: CacheDirLength 2
Default: CacheDirLength 1
Since: Apache 1.1

The directive sets the number of characters allowed in a subdirectory name in the proxy cache directory. Cached data will be saved in subdirectories of this length below CacheRoot.

■ CacheDirLevels   **mod_proxy**
Maximum Subdirectories Depth for the Proxy Document Cache
Syntax: CacheDirLevels *depth*
Example: CacheDirLevels 2
Default: CacheDirLevels 3
Since: Apache 1.1

This directive sets the number of subdirectory levels in the proxy cache directory. Cached data will be saved this many directory levels below CacheRoot.

■ CacheDefaultExpire   **mod_proxy**
Default Expiration Time for Cached Documents
Syntax: CacheDefaultExpire *hours*
Example: CacheDefaultExpire 6
Default: CacheDefaultExpure 1
Since: Apache 1.1

This directive sets the default time in hours for which the proxy server caches a document. If the document is fetched via a protocol that does not support expiration times (for instance, FTP), then the value in the *hours* argument is used as the expiration time. CacheMaxExpire does not override this setting.

■ CacheMaxExpire
mod_proxy

Maximum Expiration Time for Cached Documents
Syntax: CacheMaxExpire *hours*
Example: CacheMaxExpire 12
Default: CacheMaxExpire 24
Since: Apache 1.1

This directive sets the maximum time in hours for which the proxy server caches a document. Cachable HTTP documents will be retained for at most *hours* without checking the origin server. Thus they can be at most *hours* out of date. This restriction is enforced even if the document has its own expiration time.

■ CacheGcInterval
mod_proxy

Interval between Proxy Cache Garbage Collections
Syntax: CacheGcInterval *hours*
Example: CacheGcInterval 48
Default: CacheGcInterval 24
Since: Apache 1.1

This directive instructs the proxy server to check the document cache at the interval specified in the *hours* argument, and to delete files if the space usage exceeds that set by CacheSize. Note that the *hours* argument can contain a float value. For example, you can use "1.5" to check the cache every 90 minutes. Keep in mind that, by default, no garbage collection is performed and the cache will grow indefinitely. The larger the *hours* argument, the more extra space beyond the configured CacheSize that will be needed for the cache between garbage collections.

■ CacheLastModifiedFactor
mod_proxy

Factor Used to Estimate Expires from Last Modified HTTP Field
Syntax: CacheLastModifiedFactor *factor*
Example: CacheLastModifiedFactor 0.5
Default: CacheLastModifiedFactor 0.1
Since: Apache 1.1

This directive sets the factor that is used to estimate the Expires date from a date of the Last-Modified header field. If the origin HTTP server did not supply an expiration date for the document, then mod_proxy estimates one using the following formula: expiry-period = time-since-last-modification * *factor*. For example, if the document was last modified 10 hours ago, and *factor* is 0.1, then the expiry period will be set to 10 * 0.1 = 1 hour. If the expiry period exceeds that set by CacheMaxExpire, then the latter takes precedence.

■ CacheForceCompletion   **mod_proxy**
Completion Watermark for Canceled HTTP Transfers
Syntax: CacheForceCompletion *percentage*
Example: CacheForceCompletion 60
Default: CacheForceCompletion 90
Since: Apache 1.3

If an HTTP transfer that is being cached is canceled, mod_proxy will complete the transfer to the cache if more than the *percentage* of the data has already been transferred. This percentage must be a number between 1 and 100 (0 is the default). A value of 100 will cause a document to be cached only if the transfer was allowed to complete. Use of a number between 60 and 90 is recommended.

mod_perl
Perl Integration and Interface

■ <Perl>   **mod_perl**
Begin Perl Code Section
Syntax: <Perl>
Example: <Perl>
Default: None
Since: Apache 1.2

This directive opens a section containing a Perl program that will execute at start-up time inside a special environment. Consequently, mod_perl compiles the contents of these sections by evaluating them inside the *Apache::ReadConfig* package. After compilation is finished, mod_perl searches the symbol table of this package for global variables with the same names as Apache configuration directives. The values of those variables are then fed into Apache's normal configuration mechanism as if they had been typed directly into the configuration file.

<Perl> sections allow you to really "program" the Apache configuration in Perl syntax.

The directive is provided to help *program* the Apache configuration in Perl. For instance, you can replace redundant sections with a Perl loop. For more details about this nifty facility, refer to the chapter "Configuring Apache with Perl" in the book *Writing Apache Modules with Perl and C*.

◼ </Perl>   **mod_perl**
End Perl Code Section
Syntax: </Perl>
Example: </Perl>
Default: None
Since: Apache 1.2

Close a section previously opened by <Perl>.

◼ =pod   **mod_perl**
Begin Plain Old Document (POD) Format Section
Syntax: =pod
Example: =pod
Default: None
Since: Apache 1.2

This "convenience" directive opens a section ending with =cut that
Apache previously skipped. The intention is to allow Perl programmers to document Apache configuration files in the same way they
document Perl code. That is, the =pod and =cut directives resemble the
Perl language commands with the same names.

Use =pod and =cut to
embed documentation
in POD format.

◼ =cut   **mod_perl**
End Plain Old Document (POD) Format Section
Syntax: =cut
Example: =cut
Default: None
Since: Apache 1.2

Close a section previously opened by =pod.

◼ __END__   **mod_perl**
Stop Configuration File Parsing
Syntax: __END__
Example: __END__
Default: None
Since: Apache 1.2

Another "convenience" directive, __END__ is provided to make the lives
of Perl programmers who are using Apache configuration directives
easier. It simply stops the processing of the configuration file in the
same way that the corresponding Perl language construct marks the
end of a Perl script.

■ PerlFreshRestart   **mod_perl**
Reload of Modules and Scripts on Restarts
Syntax: `PerlFreshRestart on|off`
Example: `PerlFreshRestart on`
Default: `PerlFreshRestart off`
Since: Apache 1.2

This directive forces `mod_perl` to completely reload Perl modules (→ `PerlModule`) and scripts (→ `PerlRequire`) at every restart. As a result, changes to the start-up script and other Perl modules can take effect on restarts without the need to bring the server completely down. By default, the modules and scripts are cached even over server restarts. This default is mainly intended for developers.

■ PerlWarn   **mod_perl**
Enable Perl Warning Mode
Syntax: `PerlWarn on|off`
Example: `PerlWarn on`
Default: `PerlWarn off`
Since: Apache 1.2

This directive enables Perl's *warning* mode on start-up for all scripts that are executed under the control of `mod_perl`, but especially *Apache::-Registry* scripts. When this mode is enabled, Perl outputs various diagnostics before executing a program. See the UNIX manual page perl-diag(1), which is provided by the Perl package, for details.

■ PerlTaintCheck   **mod_perl**
Enable Perl Tainting Mode
Syntax: `PerlTaintCheck on|off`
Example: `PerlTaintCheck on`
Default: `PerlTaintCheck off`
Since: Apache 1.2

This directive enables Perl's *taint checking* on start-up for all scripts that are executed under the control of `mod_perl`, but especially *Apache::-Registry* scripts. Taint checks cause Perl to die with a fatal error if unchecked user-provided data (for instance, the values of CGI variables) are passed to a potentially dangerous function, such as `exec()`, `eval()`, or `system()`. See the UNIX manual page perlsec(1), which is provided by the Perl package, for details.

■ **PerlOpmask**   **mod_perl**

Configure Perl Operator Mask
Syntax: PerlOpmask *file*
Example: PerlOpmask conf/perl.opmask
Default: None
Since: Apache 1.2

This directive establishes a Perl operator mask that disables possibly dangerous Perl language operators. The mask is loaded from a specification in *file*. Unfortunately, to find out more details, you must look inside the mod_perl and Perl sources, because the operator mask facility is not very well documented. This facility is considered experimental and should be used only by real Perl programmers.

■ **PerlRequire**   **mod_perl**

Read and Evaluate a Perl Script
Syntax: PerlRequire *file* [*file* ...]
Example: PerlRequire /etc/httpd.init.pl
Default: None
Since: Apache 1.2

At server start-up and restart, this directive reads in and evaluates a Perl script (usually standard Perl files ending in .pl), much like Perl's built-in require command. When placed inside .htaccess files, the modules specified in the *module* arguments are loaded at HTTP request time and run under the unprivileged UID.

■ **PerlModule**   **mod_perl**

Read and Import a Perl Module
Syntax: PerlModule *module* [*module* ...]
Example: PerlModule Apache::Registry
Default: None
Since: Apache 1.2

At server start-up and restart, this directive reads in and evaluates a Perl module (usually Perl package files ending in .pm), much like Perl's built-in use command. Here *module* must be a "bare word" — that is, a package name without any file path information. When placed inside .htaccess files, the modules specified in the *module* arguments are loaded at HTTP request time and run under the unprivileged UID.

◼ PerlSetVar   **mod_perl**
Pass a Variable to Perl Modules
Syntax: PerlSetVar *variable value*
Example: PerlSetVar FooConfig conf/foo.conf
Default: None
Since: Apache 1.2

This directive passes *variable* to Perl modules. The *value* can be re-
trieved by using "dir_config ('*variable*')" on the Apache request
object. The *variable* and *value* arguments that are actually used depend on the modules, of course. Refer to the documentation of the
various *Apache::XXX* modules for details.

◼ PerlSetEnv   **mod_perl**
Pass a Variable to the SSI/CGI Environment
Syntax: PerlSetEnv *variable value*
Example: PerlSetEnv FOO_BAR Quux
Default: None
Since: Apache 1.2

This directive is similar to Apache's standard SetEnv directive; that is,
it sets *variable* to *value* inside the SSI/CGI environment. It differs from
SetEnv in that PerlSetEnv is evaluated much earlier in the HTTP processing, so that *variable* is available at an earlier point to Perl modules.

◼ PerlPassEnv   **mod_perl**
Control the Variables Passed to the SSI/CGI Environment
Syntax: PerlPassEnv *variable* [*variable* ...]
Example: PerlPassEnv FOO_BAR FOO_BAZ
Default: None
Since: Apache 1.2

This directive is similar to Apache's standard PassEnv directive; that is,
it controls which variables (set via PerlSetEnv) are actually passed to
the SSI/CGI environment. It differs from PassEnv in that PerlPassEnv
is evaluated much earlier in the HTTP processing, so that *variable* is
available at an earlier point to Perl modules.

◼ PerlSetupEnv   **mod_perl**
Tell mod_perl Whether to Set Up %ENV by Default
Syntax: PerlSetupEnv on|off
Example: PerlSetupEnv off
Default: PerlSetupEnv on
Since: Apache 1.2

This directive instructs mod_perl as to whether it should set up Perl's %ENV hash by default. Normally, mod_perl establishes %ENV automatically, but this directive can disable this behavior. This option allows you to save a few CPU cycles or to ensure that the environment isn't changed for various reasons. The environments established by mod_perl and mod_cgi can be distinguished through the value contained in the CGI environment variable GATEWAY_INTERFACE. It is set set to "CGI/1.1" by mod_cgi and to "CGI-Perl/1.1" by mod_perl.

■ PerlSendHeader   mod_perl
Scan Script's Output for HTTP Headers
Syntax: PerlSendHeader on|off
Example: PerlSendHeader off
Default: PerlSendHeader on
Since: Apache 1.2

When this directive is set to "on", it forces mod_perl to search for script output that looks like an HTTP header and automatically calls the API function send_http_header(). Turning it off saves a few CPU cycles.

■ PerlInitHandler   mod_perl
Perl Handler for the Initialization Phase
Syntax: PerlInitHandler *handler* [...]
Example: PerlInitHandler Apache::StartTimer
Default: None
Since: Apache 1.2

This directive is a special handler. When it is found outside of any <Location>, <Directory>, or <Files> sections, it serves as an alias for PerlPostReadRequestHandler. When found inside one of these containers, it serves as an alias for PerlHeaderParserHandler. Its name makes it easy to remember that this directive is the first handler invoked when serving HTTP requests. Do not mix it with the Apache module initialization phase.

■ PerlChildInitHandler   mod_perl
Perl Handler for the API Phase of Child Initialization
Syntax: PerlChildInitHandler *handler* [...]
Example: PerlChildInitHandler Apache::DBLogin
Default: None
Since: Apache 1.2

This mod_perl directive corresponds to Apache's API phase of child initialization. The *handler* argument contains the name of the subroutine to call to manage this phase. If *handler* is not a defined Perl subroutine, then mod_perl assumes it is a package name that defines a subroutine named "handler".

■ PerlPostReadRequestHandler   **mod_perl**
Perl Handler for the API Phase After HTTP Request Reading
Syntax: PerlPostReadRequestHandler *handler* [...]
Example: PerlPostReadRequestHandler Apache::Timer
Default: None
Since: Apache 1.2

This mod_perl directive corresponds to Apache's API phase of reading (but not parsing) the HTTP request. The *handler* argument contains the name of the subroutine to call to manage this phase. If *handler* is not a defined Perl subroutine, then mod_perl assumes it is a package name that defines a subroutine named "handler".

■ PerlTransHandler   **mod_perl**
Perl Handler for the API Phase of URL Translation
Syntax: PerlTransHandler *handler* [...]
Example: PerlTransHandler Apache::AdBlocker
Default: None
Since: Apache 1.2

This mod_perl directive corresponds to Apache's API phase of translating the URL to a file name. The *handler* argument contains the name of the subroutine to call to manage this phase. If *handler* is not a defined Perl subroutine, then mod_perl assumes it is a package name that defines a subroutine named "handler".

■ PerlHeaderParserHandler   **mod_perl**
Perl Handler for the API Phase of HTTP Request Parsing
Syntax: PerlHeaderParserHandler *handler* [...]
Example: PerlHeaderParserHandler Apache::Blocker
Default: None
Since: Apache 1.2

This mod_perl directive corresponds to Apache's API phase of parsing the HTTP request headers into their ingredients. The *handler* argument contains the name of the subroutine to call to manage this phase. If *handler* is not a defined Perl subroutine, then mod_perl assumes it is a package name that defines a subroutine named "handler".

■ **PerlAccessHandler**   **mod_perl**
Perl Handler for the API Phase of Host Access Checking
Syntax: PerlAccessHandler *handler* [...]
Example: PerlAccessHandler Apache::DayLimit
Default: None
Since: Apache 1.2

This mod_perl directive corresponds to Apache's API phase of host-
and network-based access checking. The *handler* argument contains
the name of the subroutine to call to manage this phase. If *handler* is
not a defined Perl subroutine, then mod_perl assumes it is a package
name that defines a subroutine named "handler".

■ **PerlAuthenHandler**   **mod_perl**
Perl Handler for the API Phase of User Authentication
Syntax: PerlAuthenHandler *handler* [...]
Example: PerlAuthenHandler Apache::AuthAnon
Default: None
Since: Apache 1.2

This mod_perl directive corresponds to Apache's API phase of user
authentication. The *handler* argument contains the name of the subroutine to call to manage this phase. If *handler* is not a defined Perl
subroutine, then mod_perl assumes it is a package name that defines a
subroutine named "handler".

■ **PerlAuthzHandler**   **mod_perl**
Perl Handler for the API Phase of User Identification
Syntax: PerlAuthzHandler *handler* [...]
Example: PerlAuthzHandler Apache::AuthzGender
Default: None
Since: Apache 1.2

This mod_perl directive corresponds to Apache's API phase of user
identification and access granting. The *handler* argument contains the
name of the subroutine to call to manage this phase. If *handler* is not
a defined Perl subroutine, then mod_perl assumes it is a package name
that defines a subroutine named "handler".

■ **PerlTypeHandler**   **mod_perl**
Perl Handler for the API Phase of MIME Type Determination
Syntax: PerlTypeHandler *handler* [...]
Example: PerlTypeHandler Apache::MimeDBI
Default: None
Since: Apache 1.2

This mod_perl directive corresponds to Apache's API phase of determining the MIME type of documents. The *handler* argument contains the name of the subroutine to call to manage this phase. If *handler* is not a defined Perl subroutine, then mod_perl assumes it is a package name that defines a subroutine named "handler".

■ PerlFixupHandler   **mod_perl**
Perl Handler for the API Phase Before the Content Handling
Syntax: PerlFixupHandler *handler* [...]
Example: PerlFixupHandler Apache::HTTP::Equiv
Default: None
Since: Apache 1.2

This mod_perl directive corresponds to Apache's API phase of fixing up the request before the content generation and delivery starts. The *handler* argument contains the name of the subroutine to call to manage this phase. If *handler* is not a defined Perl subroutine, then mod_perl assumes it is a package name that defines a subroutine named "handler."

■ PerlHandler   **mod_perl**
Perl Handler for the API Phase of Content Handling
Syntax: PerlHandler *handler* [...]
Example: PerlHandler Apache::Registry
Default: None
Since: Apache 1.3

This mod_perl directive corresponds to Apache's standard SetHandler directive. The *handler* argument contains the name of the subroutine to call to manage the content generation and delivery phase (also known as the response phase). If *handler* is not a defined Perl subroutine, then mod_perl assumes it is a package name that defines a subroutine named "handler".

■ PerlLogHandler   **mod_perl**
Perl Handler for the API Phase of Request Logging
Syntax: PerlLogHandler *handler* [...]
Example: PerlLogHandler Apache::LogMail
Default: None
Since: Apache 1.2

This mod_perl directive corresponds to Apache's API phase of logging the request. The *handler* argument contains the name of the subroutine to call to manage this phase. If *handler* is not a defined Perl subroutine, then mod_perl assumes it is a package name that defines a subroutine named "handler".

■ PerlCleanupHandler   mod_perl
Perl Handler for the API Phase of Request Cleanups
Syntax: PerlCleanupHandler *handler* [...]
Example: PerlCleanupHandler Apache::Do::cleanup
Default: None
Since: Apache 1.2

This mod_perl directive corresponds to Apache's API phase of cleaning up processing before the request handling terminates. The *handler* argument contains the name of the subroutine to call to manage this phase. If *handler* is not a defined Perl subroutine, then mod_perl assumes it is a package name that defines a subroutine named "handler".

■ PerlChildExitHandler   mod_perl
Perl Handler for the API Phase of Child Exits
Syntax: PerlChildExitHandler *handler* [...]
Example: PerlChildExitHandler Apache::DBLogout
Default: None
Since: Apache 1.2

This mod_perl directive corresponds to Apache's API phase of child termination. The *Handler* argument contains the name of the subroutine to call to manage this phase. If *handler* is not a defined Perl subroutine, then mod_perl assumes it is a package name that defines a subroutine named "handler".

■ PerlDispatchHandler   mod_perl
Perl Handler for the Pseudo-API Phase of Dispatching Handlers
Syntax: PerlDispatchHandler *handler* [...]
Example: PerlDispatchHandler MyDispatch::handler
Default: None
Since: Apache 1.2

This special Perl handler does not correspond to a real Apache API phase. Instead, it configures *handler* to take over the process of loading and executing handler code. That is, instead of processing the Perl*Handler directives directly, mod_perl invokes *handler* and passes it the Apache request and the handler that would ordinarily be invoked to process this phase. The *handler* argument always contains the name of a Perl subroutine rather than just a Perl module name.

■ PerlRestartHandler   **mod_perl**

Perl Handler for the Pseudo-API Phase of Server Restarts

Syntax: PerlRestartHandler *handler* [...]

Example: PerlRestartHandler MyRestart::handler

Default: None

Since: Apache 1.2

This special Perl handler does not correspond to a real Apache API phase. Instead, it configures *handler* to operate when the Apache server is restarted. You then have the chance to step in and perform any cleanup required to tweak the Perl interpreter.

mod_ssl
SSL/TLS Integration and Interface

■ SSLPassPhraseDialog   **mod_ssl**

Type of Pass Phrase Dialog for Encrypted Private Keys

Syntax: SSLPassPhraseDialog *type*

Example: SSLPassPhraseDialog exec:bin/fetchphrase

Default: SSLPassPhraseDialog builtin

Since: Apache 1.3

When Apache starts up, mod_ssl must read the various certificate ($\rightarrow$ SSLCertificateFile) and private key ($\rightarrow$ SSLCertificateKeyFile) files of the SSL-enabled virtual servers. For security reasons, the private key files are usually encrypted. Consequently, mod_ssl needs to query the administrator for a *pass phrase* to decrypt those files. The *type* argument specifies the approach taken for this query: "builtin" means that an interactive terminal dialog is used; "exec:*filepath*" means that *filepath* executes and provides the *pass phrase* on stdout.

■ SSLMutex   **mod_ssl**

Semaphore for Internal Mutual Exclusion of Operations

Syntax: SSLMutex *type*

Example: SSLMutex file:logs/ssl_mutex

Default: SSLMutex none

Since: Apache 1.3

This directive configures the SSL engine's global semaphore, which is used for mutual exclusion of operations that must be carried out in a synchronized way between the pre-forked Apache server processes. This directive can be used only in the global server context, because one global mutex is needed. The *type* argument can be either "none" for no mutex (risky but works for most situations) or "file:*filepath*" for using a *lock file* on the file system. On some platforms, a third variant, "sem", is available that uses a SysV IPC Semaphore (under UNIX) or a Windows Mutex (under Win32).

■ SSLRandomSeed   mod_ssl
Pseudo-Random Number Generator (PRNG) Seeding Source
Syntax: SSLRandomSeed *context source* [*bytes*]
Example: SSLRandomSeed startup builtin
Default: None
Since: Apache 1.3

This directive configures one or more sources for seeding the *Pseudo-Random Number Generator* (PRNG) in *OpenSSL* at start-up (*context* is "startup") or just before a new SSL connection is established (*context* is "connect"). It can be used only in the global server context, because PRNG is a global facility. Several *source* variants are available. The "builtin" option uses an existing internal seeding source that consumes minimal CPU cycles under runtime and hence can be used without drawbacks.

> Make sure to configure reasonable SSLRandomSeed directives in order to allow OpenSSL to have enough entropy available for its cryptography algorithms to work securely.

In the "file:*filepath*" option, the seeding data are read from *filepath*, which is especially interesting with an existing /dev/urandom device. The *source* argument can also take the form "exec:*filepath*", where *filepath* is treated as a program that is executed and the seeding data are read from its stdout. Optionally, a *bytes* argument can be given that forces mod_ssl to read only the specified amount of data instead of all data until end of file is reached.

■ SSLSessionCache   mod_ssl
Type of the Global/Interprocess SSL Session Cache
Syntax: SSLSessionCache *type*
Example: SSLSessionCache dbm:logs/ssl_cache
Default: SSLSessionCache none
Since: Apache 1.3

This directive configures the storage type of the global/interprocess SSL *session cache*. This cache speeds up parallel request processing by avoiding unnecessary session handshakes on subsequent or even parallel requests. Three storage *type*s are supported: "none" disables the session cache (not recommended); "dbm:*filepath*" uses a UNIX NDBM file on disk (under *filepath*) as the cache storage (the portable cache variant); and "shm:*filepath*[(*bytes*)]" uses a high-performance hash table inside a shared memory segment as the cache storage (the shared memory segment is established via *filepath* and has a maximum size of *bytes*).

> Use "SSLSessionCache shm" in conjunction with the MM shared memory library to achieve maximum runtime performance for the HTTPS protocol.

■ SSLSessionCacheTimeout   **mod_ssl**
Seconds Before a Session Expires in the SSL Session Cache
Syntax: SSLSessionCacheTimeout *seconds*
Example: SSLSessionCacheTimeout 1200
Default: SSLSessionCacheTimeout 300
Since: Apache 1.3

This directive sets the timeout in *seconds* for the information stored
in the global/interprocess SSL *session cache* ($\rightarrow$ SSLSessionCache) and
the *OpenSSL* internal memory cache. It can be set as low as "15" for
testing purposes, but should be set to values such as "300" or higher
for real-world applications.

■ SSLEngine   **mod_ssl**
SSL Engine Operation Switch
Syntax: SSLEngine on|off
Example: SSLEngine on
Default: SSLEngine off
Since: Apache 1.3

This directive toggles the usage of the SSL/TLS protocol engine. It is
typically employed inside a <VirtualHost> section to enable SSL/TLS
for a particular virtual host. By default, the SSL/TLS protocol engine
is disabled for both the main server and all configured virtual hosts.

■ SSLProtocol   **mod_ssl**
Configure Usable SSL Protocol Flavors
Syntax: SSLProtocol [+|-]*protocol* [...]
Example: SSLProtocol all -SSLv2
Default: SSLProtocol all
Since: Apache 1.3

This directive controls the SSL/TLS protocol flavors that mod_ssl uses
when establishing its server environment. Clients can connect only
with one of the configured protocols. The available (case-insensitive)
protocol strings are "SSLv2", "SSLv3", "TLSv1", and "All". All these
strings can also be combined by using positive ("+") and negative ("-")
prefixes.

■ SSLCipherSuite   **mod_ssl**
SSL Cipher Suite for Negotiation in SSL Handshake Phase
Syntax: SSLCipherSuite *cipher-spec*
Example: SSLCipherSuite ALL:!RSA
Default: SSLCipherSuite ALL:+HIGH:+MEDIUM:+LOW
Since: Apache 1.3

This complex directive uses a colon-separated *cipher-spec* string consisting of *OpenSSL* cipher specifications to configure the *cipher suite* that the client negotiates in the SSL handshake phase. It can be used in either per-server or per-directory context. In per-server context, it applies to the standard SSL handshake when a connection is established. In per-directory context, it forces an SSL renegotiation with the reconfigured cipher suite after the HTTP request is read but before the HTTP response is sent. The complete syntax of *cipher-spec* appears in the mod_ssl manual. To list the available ciphers, use the "openssl ciphers -v" command.

Use SSLCipherSuite to control the ciphers the client is allowed to negotiate with your web server on HTTPS requests.

■ **SSLCertificateFile** **mod_ssl**
Server PEM-Encoded X.509 Certificate File
Syntax: SSLCertificateFile *file*
Example: SSLCertificateFile etc/ssl/host.crt
Default: None
Since: Apache 1.3

This directive points with *file* to the PEM-encoded *certificate* file for the server and, optionally, to the corresponding RSA or DSA *private key* file for it (contained in the same file). If the private key is encrypted, the *pass phrase* dialog (→ SSLPassPhraseDialog) is forced at start-up time. This directive can be used a maximum of two times (referencing different file names) when both RSA- and DSA-based server certificates are used in parallel.

■ **SSLCertificateKeyFile** **mod_ssl**
Server PEM-Encoded Private Key File
Syntax: SSLCertificateKeyFile *file*
Example: SSLCertificateKeyFile etc/ssl/host.key
Default: None
Since: Apache 1.3

This directive points with *file* to the PEM-encoded RSA or DSA *private key* file for the server. If the private key is not combined with the *Certificate* in SSLCertificateFile, use this directive to point to the file with the stand-alone private key. If SSLCertificateFile is used and the file contains both the certificate and the private key, this directive is unnecessary. We strongly discourage this practice. For security reasons, we recommend separating the certificate and the private key. If the private key is encrypted, the *pass phrase* dialog (→ SSLPassPhraseDialog) is forced at start-up. This directive can be used a maximum of two times (referencing different file names) when both RSA- and DSA-based private keys are used in parallel.

■ SSLCACertificatePath   mod_ssl
Directory of PEM-Encoded CA Certificates for Client Authentication
Syntax: SSLCACertificatePath *directory*
Example: SSLCACertificatePath etc/ssl/
Default: None
Since: Apache 1.3

This directive sets the *directory* where you keep the certificates of *certi-fication authorities* (CAs) of those clients with which you deal. It is used to verify the client certificate during *client authentication*. The files in this directory must be PEM-encoded and are accessed through hash file names. Typically, you have to place the certificate files there and then create symbolic links with the help of the Makefile in the ssl.crt/ directory that comes with mod_ssl to accomplish this task.

■ SSLCACertificateFile   mod_ssl
File of PEM-Encoded CA Certificates for Client Authentication
Syntax: SSLCACertificateFile *file*
Example: SSLCACertificateFile etc/ssl/all.crt
Default: None
Since: Apache 1.3

This directive sets the *all-in-one file* where you can assemble the certifi-cates of the *certification authorities* of those clients with which you deal. These certificates are used for *client authentication*. The file is simply the concatenation of the various PEM-encoded certificate files, placed in order of preference. This directive can be used as an alternative to or in conjunction with SSLCACertificatePath.

■ SSLCARevocationPath   mod_ssl
Directory of PEM-Encoded CA Certificate Revocation Lists (CRL)
Syntax: SSLCARevocationPath *directory*
Example: SSLCARevocationPath etc/ssl/
Default: None
Since: Apache 1.3

This directive sets the *directory* where you keep the X.509 *certificate re-vocation lists* (CRLs) of *certification authorities*, which are used to reject revoked certificates. The files in this directory must be PEM-encoded and are accessed through hash file names. Typically, you have to place the CRL files there and then create symbolic links with the help of the Makefile in the ssl.crl/ directory that comes with mod_ssl to accom-plish this task.

■ SSLCARevocationFile   mod_ssl
File of PEM-Encoded CA Certificate Revocation Lists (CRL)
Syntax: SSLCARevocationFile *file*
Example: SSLCARevocationFile etc/ssl/all.crl
Default: None
Since: Apache 1.3

This directive sets the *all-in-one file* where you can assemble the certificate revocation lists of *certification authorities,* which are used to reject revoked certificates. Such a file is simply the concatenation of the various PEM-encoded CRL files, placed in order of preference. This directive can be used as an alternative to or in conjunction with SSLCARevocationPath.

■ SSLVerifyClient   mod_ssl
Type of Client Certificate Verification
Syntax: SSLVerifyClient *type*
Example: SSLVerifyClient require
Default: SSLVerifyClient none
Since: Apache 1.3

This directive sets the certificate verification *type* for *client authentication.* Notice that it can be used in either per-server or per-directory context. In per-server context, it applies to the client authentication process used in the standard SSL handshake when a connection is established. In per-directory context, it forces an SSL renegotiation with the reconfigured client verification level after the HTTP request is read but before the HTTP response is sent.

Use SSLVerifyClient to provide client authentication via X.509 certificates.

The following *type* variants are possible: "none" where no client certificate is required; "optional" where the client *may* present a valid certificate; "require" where the client *must* present a valid certificate; and "optional_no_ca" where the client may present a valid certificate but does not have to in order to be (successfully) verifiable.

■ SSLVerifyClientDepth   mod_ssl
Maximum Depth of CA Certificates in Client Certificate Verification
Syntax: SSLVerifyClientDepth *depth*
Example: SSLVerifyClientDepth 10
Default: SSLVerifyClientDepth 1
Since: Apache 1.3

This directive dictates how deeply mod_ssl should go before deciding that a client does not have a valid certificate. It can be used in either per-server or per-directory context. In per-server context, it applies to the client authentication process used in the standard SSL handshake when a connection is established. In per-directory context, it forces an SSL renegotiation with the reconfigured client verification depth after the HTTP request is read but before the HTTP response is sent.

The *depth* is the maximum number of intermediate certificate issuers — that is, the maximum number of CA certificates that can be followed while verifying the client certificate. A depth of 0 means that only self-signed client certificates are accepted. The default depth of 1 means that the client certificate can be self-signed or signed by a CA that is directly known to the server (for example, the CA's certificate under SSLCACertificatePath).

■ **SSLLog**   **mod_ssl**
Location in Which to Write the Dedicated SSL Engine Log File
Syntax: SSLLog *file*
Example: SSLLog logs/ssl_engine_log
Default: None
Since: Apache 1.3

This directive sets the *file* of the dedicated SSL protocol engine log file. Error-type messages are also duplicated to the general Apache error log file ($\rightarrow$ ErrorLog). This directive should appear where it cannot be used for symbolic link attacks on a real server (that is, somewhere that only the "root" can write). If the file name does not begin with a slash ("/"), then it is assumed to be relative to the *server root*. If *file* begins with a bar ("|"), then the following string is assumed to be a file path to an executable program to which a reliable pipe can be established.

■ **SSLLogLevel**   **mod_ssl**
Logging Level for the Dedicated SSL Engine Log File
Syntax: SSLLogLevel *level*
Example: SSLLogLevel trace
Default: SSLLogLevel none
Since: Apache 1.3

Always use
"SSLLogLevel error"
on production servers
to avoid performance
penalties, but use
"SSLLogLevel trace"
for a convenient way to
debug the HTTPS
processing.

This directive sets the verbosity degree of the dedicated SSL protocol engine log file ($\rightarrow$ SSLLog). The *level* argument can have any of several values (listed here in ascending order, where higher levels include lower levels). The "none" option means that no dedicated SSL logging is written, but messages of level "error" are written to the general Apache error log file. The "error" option logs messages of the error type only — that is, messages that show fatal situations (processing is usually stopped). Those messages are also duplicated to the general Apache error log file.

The "warn" option logs warning messages, which show non-fatal problems (processing is usually continued). The "info" option logs informational messages, which show major processing steps. The "trace" option logs trace messages, messages that show minor processing steps. Finally, the "debug" option logs debugging messages, which show development and low-level I/O information.

■ SSLOptions   mod_ssl
Configure SSL Engine Runtime Options
Syntax: SSLOptions [+|-]*option* [...]
Example: SSLOptions +FakeBasicAuth -CompatEnvVars
Default: None
Since: Apache 1.3

This directive controls various runtime options on a per-directory basis. Normally, if multiple SSLOptions could apply to a directory, then the most specific one is taken completely; that is,the options are not merged. If all options on the SSLOptions directive are preceded by a plus ("+") or minus ("-") symbol, however, then they are merged. Any options preceded by a "+" are added to the options currently in force, and any options preceded by a "-" are removed from the options currently in force.

The *option*s argument may have several values. "CompatEnvVars" exports additional SSI/CGI environment variables for backward-compatibility reasons. "ExportCertData" exports the client and server certificates in PEM format to the SSI/CGI environment. "FakeBasicAuth" enables the translation of the *Subject Distinguished Name* of the client X.509 certificate into an HTTP *Basic Authorization* user name. "StrictRequire" *forces* forbidden access when SSLRequireSSL or SSLRequire successfully decides that access should be forbidden even when a "Satisfy any" option is active.

■ SSLRequireSSL   mod_ssl
Deny Access When SSL Is Not Used for the HTTP Request
Syntax: SSLRequireSSL
Example: SSLRequireSSL
Default: None
Since: Apache 1.3

This directive forbids access unless HTTP over SSL (that is, HTTPS) is enabled for the current connection. It is very handy inside the SSL-enabled virtual host or directories as a defense against configuration errors that expose data that should be protected. When this directive is present, all requests that do not use SSL are denied.

■ **SSLRequire**   **mod_ssl**

Allow Access Only When a Boolean Expression Is True

Syntax: SSLRequire *expression*

Example: SSLRequire %{SSL_CIPHER} !~ m/↑EXP-/

Default: None

Since: Apache 1.3

This directive specifies a general access requirement that must be ful-
filled to allow access. It is a very powerful directive because the *expression* is an arbitrarily complex Boolean expression containing any
number of access checks. See the mod_ssl user manual for more details.

Use SSLRequire for
fine-grained HTTPS
access control.

Chapter **5**

Running Apache

/O, /Ot Minimize execution speed (default)
— Microsoft Visual C/C++ documentation,
"Environment and Tools," p. 531

N ow that we have discussed in detail how Apache has been built and configured, it is time to actually run it. In this short chapter, we present the third reference part: the available command-line options of both the Apache daemon program and the Apache control program.

5.1 Command-Line Reference

5.1.1 Apache Daemon Program

This section presents a complete reference to the command line of the Apache daemon program. Because we built Apache with "`--target=apache`" in Chapter 3 on page 37, the Apache program is named `apache`. By default, it is usually called `httpd` for historical reasons. The command line has the following general structure:

```
$ apache [ option ... ]
```

The following *option*s are available on the Apache command line.

■ **-R** *libexecdir*   DSO Runtime Path

This option is available only if Apache was built with the SHARED_CORE rule enabled, which forces the Apache core code to be placed into a Dynamic Shared Object (DSO) file. By default, this file is searched in a hard-coded path under ServerRoot. Use this option if you want to override the default.

■ **-d** *serverroot*   Server Root Directory

This option sets the initial value for the ServerRoot directory to *serverroot*. It can be overridden by the ServerRoot directive in the configuration file. The default is /usr/local/apache.

■ **-f** *configfile*   Server Configuration File

This option executes the commands in the file *configfile* on start-up. If *configfile* does not begin with a slash character ("/"), then it is taken to be a path relative to ServerRoot. The default is conf/httpd.conf.

■ **-C** *directive*   Extra Configuration Directive Prolog

This option processes the configuration *directive* before reading the configuration files.

■ **-c** *directive*   Extra Configuration Directive Epilog

This option processes the configuration *directive* after reading the configuration files.

■ **-D** *parameter*   Define a Configuration Parameter

This option sets a configuration *parameter* that can be used with <IfDefine> sections in the configuration files to conditionally skip or process commands.

■ **-h**   Output Help Page

This option outputs a short summary of available command-line options.

■ **-l**   Output List of Built-in Modules

This option outputs a list of modules compiled into the server.

■ **-L**   Output List of Implemented Directives

This option outputs a list of directives together with expected arguments and places where the directive is valid.

■ **-S**   Show Virtual Host Settings

This option shows the settings as parsed from the configuration file (currently, it shows the only virtual host settings).

■ **-t**   Test Configuration Contents

This option runs syntax tests for the configuration files only. The program immediately exits after this syntax parsing, with either a return code of 0 (syntax OK) or a return code not equal to 0 (syntax error).

■ **-X**   Run in Single-Process Mode

This option runs in single-process mode, for internal debugging purposes only; the daemon does not detach from the terminal or fork any children. Do *not* use this mode to provide ordinary web service.

■ **-v**   Output Version Information

This option prints the version of Apache and then exits.

■ **-V**   Output Version and Build Information

This option prints the version and build parameters of Apache and then exits.

5.1.2 Apache Control Program

For convenience, an optional front end named apachectl (for "Apache Control") exists that can be used for easy starting, restarting, and even stopping of Apache. This script has the following general command-line structure:

```
$ apachectl [ command ... ]
```

The following *command*s are available on the Apache control command line:

■ **start**   Start Apache

This command starts the Apache daemon and gives an error if it is already running.

■ **stop**   Stop Apache

This command stops the Apache daemon.

■ **restart**   Restart Apache

This command restarts the Apache daemon by sending it a SIGHUP. If the daemon is not running, it is started. The command automatically checks the configuration files via configtest before initiating the restart to make sure Apache doesn't die.

■ **fullstatus**   Display Status

This command displays a full status report from mod_status. For it to work, you must have mod_status enabled on your server and a text-based browser such as lynx available on your system. The URL used to access the status report is /server-status.

■ **status**   Display Status

This command displays a brief status report. It is similar to the fullstatus command, except that it omits the list of requests currently being served.

■ **graceful**   Graceful Restart Apache

This command gracefully restarts the Apache daemon by sending it a
SIGUSR1. If the daemon is not running, it is started. This procedure
differs from a normal restart in that currently open connections are
not aborted. A side effect is that old log files are not closed immediately. Consequently, if this command is used in a log rotation script, a
substantial delay may be necessary to ensure that the old log files are
closed before processing them. The command automatically checks the
configuration files via configtest before initiating the restart to make
sure Apache doesn't die.

■ **configtest**   Test Configuration

This command runs a configuration file syntax test. It parses the configuration files and reports either "Syntax Ok" or detailed information
about the particular syntax error.

■ **help**   Display Help Page

This command displays a short help message.

Chapter **6**

Apache Resources

Apache, like UNIX, was not designed to stop people from doing stupid things with it, because that would also stop them from doing clever things with it.

— Unknown (paraphrased)

This chapter lists selected resources from the Apache world. The number of Apache-related projects on the Internet is very large, so only the essential ones are included here. The goal is to present you with only the most important and stable entry points, rather than a comprehensive list. The Apache world changes daily, so a very concise list of entry points to reach the latest news about Apache and further details on technical issues will prove more useful than an all-in-one list.

6.1   Online Resources

The first and most interesting group of resources are those you can find directly on the Internet. They may provide the latest news, but are usually not very concise. Nevertheless, they should be your primary entry point to the Apache world.

6.1.1   Apache Itself

Three major locations deal directly with Apache: the Apache Software Foundation, the Apache HTTP server project, and the Apache Conference (Apache-Con):

- **Apache Software Foundation (ASF)**

  `http://www.apache.org/`

  The home page of the Apache Software Foundation, a nonprofit organization representing the Apache Group. Whenever you are dealing with an Apache-related project, license, sponsoring, or press issues, go to this site. It is under direct control of the Apache Group's board of trustees (a subset of the Apache Group's developer core team) and is located in San Francisco, California.

- **Apache HTTP Server Project (Apache)**

  `http://www.apache.org/httpd`

  The home page of the *Apache HTTP server project*, also known as "The Apache." Here you can find official information about the Apache web server. Any new Apache release is announced on this site. Whenever a security problem occurs, you can find the details (and fixes) there. The site also provides information about the people behind Apache. It is under direct control of the Apache Group core team and is located in San Francisco, California.

- **Apache Annual Conference (ApacheCon)**

  `http://www.apachecon.com/`

  The web site of ApacheCon, the annual conference dedicated to Apache. When you attend ApacheCon, refer to this resource to obtain the conference agenda and other background information. It's under control of the Apache Group and the company managing the next conference.

6.1.2   Apache News

To keep informed about current events in the Apache market, visit at least the following two web sites on a regular basis.

- **ApacheWeek**

  `http://www.apacheweek.com/`

  The primary source for weekly Apache news. When you want to follow Apache developments, visit these sites on a regular basis. You will get concise overviews of the latest source changes and issues from the *new-httpd@apache.org* mailing list. This web site is located in London,

United Kingdom, and provided by Mark J. Cox. Mark is a member of the *Apache Software Foundation* and an Apache developer. Some important topics covered in ApacheWeek issues have evolved into interesting stand-alone feature articles. Watch for those on the ApacheWeek site, too.

▪ O'Reilly Apache DevCenter
http://www.oreillynet.com/apache/

A resource location for Apache developers provided by the O'Reilly & Associates Network. Here you can find additional documentation and articles related to Apache.

▪ ApacheToday
http://apachetoday.com/

A news site provided by the internet.com Corp. for the Apache community. Here one can find new feature articles about Apache on a regular basis.

▪ Slashdot Apache Section
http://slashdot.org/index.pl?section=apache

One of the most popular news sites for hackers. It includes a section dedicated to Apache, where you can find all types of weekly news and discussions of hot topics. If you want to read user opinions, look there. The site is moderated by Jim Jagielski, an Apache developer.

▪ Netcraft Server Survey
http://www.netcraft.com/survey/

A commercial company that summarizes the web server market on a monthly basis by analyzing and accumulating the HTTP Server response headers of more than 4 million web sites. The results are impressive, showing that Apache owns more than half of the web server market (and is leaving Microsoft and Netscape servers behind). This site is located the United Kingdom.

▪ E-Soft, Inc. Server Survey
http://www.securityspace.com/s_survey/

Another commercial company that summarizes the web server market on a monthly basis. It also provides statistics about the various Apache modules and their community and evolution.

6.1.3   Apache Support

If you need support for Apache, check the following resources.

■ **USENET Newsgroup c.i.w.s.u**
`news:comp.infosystems.www.servers.unix`

The primary Apache support forum on the Internet. If you are an Apache user and have a question, ask it here first. If you do not have access to USENET directly, you can reach the newsgroups through Deja (see `http://deja.com/`) or similar access services.

■ **Apache Support Companies and Contractors**
`http://www.apache.org/info/support.cgi`

This is a list of other officially known companies and contractors providing commercial support for Apache.

■ **Apache 1st**
`http://www.apache1st.com/`

Apache1st is a commercial service from *Covalent Technologies* for expert Apache support.

6.1.4   Apache Documentation

Plenty of documentation, articles, papers, and other texts for Apache are flying around on the Internet. Most of this information, however, derives from the following locations.

■ **Apache Documentation and F.A.Q. List**
`http://www.apache.org/docs/`
`http://www.apache.org/docs/misc/FAQ.html`

The primary online resource for Apache documentation. Here you can always find the latest set of HTML pages describing the Apache web server parts. The site provides an always up-to-date, checked-out version of the Apache documentation from the source repository. It is the definitive reference and authority.

■ **Apache API Dictionary**
`http://dev.apache.org/apidoc/`

This is a complete reference for the *Application Programming Interface* (API) of the Apache server.

■ **Apache Reference**
`http://www.apacheref.com/`

The accompanying web site to *Apache Desktop Reference* (the book you are currently reading). Here you can find the electronic version of the entire book, errata, and other updated material. It also provides online the complete reference of the Apache configuration directives.

■ **Apache Quick Reference Card**
http://www.refcards.com/about/apache.html

A very concise and tiny reference card for the Apache web server. It is also available in print form from O'Reilly & Associates, but the online version is always more up-to-date.

■ **Apache Developer Site**
http://dev.apache.org/

When you participate in Apache development (by writing an extension module) or just want to learn technical background information about the Apache release cycle, the Apache Group's voting guidelines, and other aspects of Apache, this site is for you. It's a horrible mess in terms of content and style, but nevertheless has a few interesting things for people working with and on Apache.

6.1.5 Apache Modules

As shipped, Apache is a very powerful web server. Nevertheless, plenty of additional modules are available to extend the web server. The following are the most important references.

■ **Apache Module Registry**
http://modules.apache.org/

A site containing references to most existing Apache modules. It should be your first entry point when you search for an Apache module or a particular functionality that is already implemented by a module. It's provided by Covalent in Lincoln, Nebraska and is under the personal control of Randy Terbush, an Apache developer.

■ **mod_perl**
http://perl.apache.org/

Doug MacEachern's popular integration of the Perl language into Apache. It can be used for Perl-based, server-side scripting; for persistent and fast CGI-like programming; and even for programming your own Apache modules in Perl. This module provides most of the Apache API in Perl.

▪ **mod_php**
   `http://www.php.net/`

   Rasmus Lerdorf's popular server-side scripting language, PHP. One of the killer modules for Apache, it is a de facto standard for creating dynamic content with Apache.

▪ **mod_jserv**
   `http://java.apache.org/`

   The Java Servlet Engine module for Apache. It allows you to run Java servlets under Apache. This project also includes Java-related subprojects.

▪ **mod_dav**
   `http://www.webdav.org/mod_dav/`

   The WebDAV module from Greg Stein. It provides the functionality of the Distributed Authoring and Versioning (DAV) standard to Apache. DAV is the forthcoming standard for manipulating documents on a web server through HTTP.

▪ **mod_ssl**
   `http://www.modssl.org/`

   The Apache interface to OpenSSL created by Ralf S. Engelschall, the author of this book. This module integrates the Secure Sockets Layer (SSL) and Transfer Layer Security (TLS) protocols into Apache with the help of the SSL/TLS toolkit OpenSSL. SSL/TLS is the de facto standard for secure communications between web browsers and servers.

6.2   Print Resources

The second most important source for Apache information includes print resources — that is, books about Apache. This section gives a quick overview of selected references to help you make your decision for a companion book more easily.

6.2.1   Apache Developer Books

The following books are intended for developers.

▪ **Writing Apache Modules with Perl and C** (1st ed.)
   Authors: Lincoln Stein, Doug MacEachern
   Published by: O'Reilly & Associates, 1999
   Companion web site: `http://www.apachemod.com/`

ISBN: 1-56592-567-X
Language: English
Pages: 725

■ **Apache Server Commentary** (1st ed.)
Authors: Greg Holden, Matthew Keller, Nick Wells
Published by: The Coriolis Group, 1999
Companion web site: none
ISBN: 1-57610-468-0
Language: English
Pages: 592

6.2.2   Apache User Books

The following books are intended mainly for users. References to more (especially older) books of this type can be found under `http://www.apache-.org/info/apache_books.html`.

■ **Apache Pocket Reference** (1st ed.)
Author: Andrew Ford
Published by: O'Reilly & Associates, 2000
Companion web site: none
ISBN: 1-56592-706-0
Language: English
Pages: 108

■ **Apache Desktop Reference** (1st ed.)
Author: Ralf S. Engelschall
Published by: Addison-Wesley, 2000
Companion web site: `http://www.apacheref.com/`
ISBN: 0-201-60470-1
Language: English
Pages: 180

■ **Apache Server Unleashed** (1st ed.)
Authors: Bowen, Coar, Grip-Jansson, Kozlov, Tuñon, Marlowe
Published by: Sams Publishing, 2000
Companion web site: `http://apacheunleashed.com/`
ISBN: 0-672-31808-3
Language: English
Pages: 656

■ **Apache Web-Server** (3rd ed.)
Author: Lars Eilebrecht
Published by: MITP-Verlag GmbH, 2000

Companion web site: none
ISBN: 3-8266-0612-4
Language: German
Pages: 600

■ **Apache Administrator's Handbook** (1st ed.)
Author: Mohammed J. Kabir
Published by: IDG Books Worldwide, 1999
Companion web site: none
ISBN: 0-7645-3306-1
Language: English
Pages: 550

■ **Apache — The Definitive Guide** (2nd ed.)
Authors: Ben Laurie, Peter Laurie
Published by: O'Reilly & Associates, 1999
Companion web site: none
ISBN: 1-56592-528-9 (en), 3-89721-127-0 (de)
Language: English or German
Pages: 370

■ **Professional Apache** (1st ed.)
Authors: P. Wainwright, L. Eilebrecht, A. Halberstadt, B. Moon
Published by: Wrox Press Ltd., 1999
Companion web site: none
ISBN: 1-861003-02-1
Language: English
Pages: 800

■ **Apache Server for Dummies** (1st ed.)
Author: Ken Coar
Published by: IDG Books Worldwide, 1998
Companion web site: `http://apache-server.com/`
ISBN: 0-7645-0291-3
Language: English
Pages: 350

6.3 Apache-Related Standards

The third resource for Apache are the related protocol and system standards.

6.3.1 Hypertext Transfer Protocol (HTTP)

The *Hypertext Transfer Protocol* is the workhorse of the World Wide Web. You can find general information about HTTP at the home of the *IETF Hypertext Transfer Protocol (HTTP) Working Group* on `http://www.ics.uci.edu/-pub/ietf/http/`. The most important references are provided here.

- **Hypertext Transfer Protocol, Version 0.9 (HTTP/0.9)**
  The original HTTP version as defined in 1991 by the World Wide Web initiative prototype software and extended in 1992. This version is still supported by Apache but its use has been strongly deprecated.
  `http://www.w3.org/Protocols/HTTP/AsImplemented.html`
  `http://www.w3.org/Protocols/HTTP/HTTP2.html`

- **Hypertext Transfer Protocol, Version 1.0 (HTTP/1.0)**
  The first really standardized and complete HTTP version as defined in 1996 as Request For Comments (RFC) 1945. This version, which is fully supported by Apache, is the version used by most browsers.
  `ftp://ftp.isi.edu/in-notes/rfc1954.txt`

- **Hypertext Transfer Protocol, Version 1.1 (HTTP/1.1)**
  The third generation of HTTP as defined in 1997 as RFC (p.171) 2068 and updated in 1999 by RFC (p.171) 2616. This version is fully supported by Apache when acting as an origin server (the usual case), but only partially supported when acting as a proxy server. [1] This HTTP version is not fully supported by all browsers. [2]
  `ftp://ftp.isi.edu/in-notes/rfc2068.txt`
  `ftp://ftp.isi.edu/in-notes/rfc2616.txt`

- **Use and Interpretation of HTTP Version Numbers**
  An informational RFC that describes the proper use and interpretation of HTTP version numbers in HTTP request and response messages.

---

[1] The original design of Apache's proxy module (`mod_proxy`) doesn't allow the implementation of some HTTP/1.1 features like *Keep-Alive connections*. Also, to fulfil the proxy-related caching requirements of HTTP/1.1, much programming effort would be needed, which isn't reasonable. Thus, for Apache 2.0, a complete rewrite of the proxy module is a must.

[2] Current browsers usually support HTTP/1.0 with a few extensions borrowed from HTTP/1.1, like the `Host` header. They usually do not support the full HTTP/1.1 protocol.

This RFC is a companion to the HTTP standards.
`ftp://ftp.isi.edu/in-notes/rfc2145.txt`

6.3.2   Uniform Resource Identifier (URI)

Uniform Resource Identifiers are the addresses of the World Wide Web. You can find general information about them at the home of the *IETF Uniform Resource Identifiers (URI) Working Group* at `http://www.ics.uci.edu/pub-/ietf/uri/`. References to the most prominent variant, the *Uniform Resource Locators (URL)*, are present here.

- **Uniform Resource Identifiers (URI): Generic Syntax**
  `ftp://ftp.isi.edu/in-notes/rfc2396.txt`, 1998

- **Uniform Resource Locators (URL)**
  `ftp://ftp.isi.edu/in-notes/rfc1738.txt`, 1994

- **Relative Uniform Resource Locators**
  `ftp://ftp.isi.edu/in-notes/rfc1808.txt`, 1995

6.3.3   Other Important Standards

- **Common Gateway Protocol, Version 1.1 (CGI/1.1)**
  `http://hoohoo.ncsa.uiuc.edu/cgi/interface.html`

- **World Wide Web Distributed Authoring and Versioning (WebDAV)**
  `http://www.ics.uci.edu/pub/ietf/webdav/`

- **Transport Layer Security, Version 1.0 (TLS/1.0)**
  `ftp://ftp.isi.edu/in-notes/rfc2246.txt`

- **IANA Assigned Numbers**
  `http://www.iana.org/`
  `ftp://ftp.isi.edu/in-notes/std/std2.txt`

- **Multipurpose Internet Mail Extensions (MIME)**
  The MIME standard describes the format of Internet message bodies. It is related to Apache in that HTTP request and response messages use MIME format for representing at least the headers.
  `ftp://ftp.isi.edu/in-notes/rfc2045.txt`
  `ftp://ftp.isi.edu/in-notes/rfc2046.txt`
  `ftp://ftp.isi.edu/in-notes/rfc2047.txt`
  `ftp://ftp.isi.edu/in-notes/rfc2048.txt`
  `ftp://ftp.isi.edu/in-notes/rfc2049.txt`

Index

This book was typeset in Europe by the author on the UNIX operating system FreeBSD 4.2 with the typesetting system $\TeX$ and its macro language $\LaTeX 2_\varepsilon$. It was designed for U.S.-letter paper ($8\frac{1}{2}in. \times 11in.$) with crop marks at $7\frac{3}{8}in. \times 9\frac{1}{4}in.$ for reproduction. It is typeset in the 10pt *Adobe Palatino* font family. It was shipped to the publisher in camera-ready *Postscript* format via the Internet.

Register
Your Book
at www.aw.com/cseng/register

You may be eligible to receive:
- Advance notice of forthcoming editions of the book
- Related book recommendations
- Chapter excerpts and supplements of forthcoming titles
- Information about special contests and promotions throughout the year
- Notices and reminders about author appearances, tradeshows, and online chats with special guests

Contact us

If you are interested in writing a book or reviewing manuscripts prior to publication, please write to us at:

Editorial Department
Addison-Wesley Professional
75 Arlington Street, Suite 300
Boston, MA 02116 USA
Email: AWPro@aw.com

Visit us on the Web: http://www.aw.com/cseng